FROM THE SOIL

FROM THE SOIL

THE FOUNDATIONS OF
CHINESE SOCIETY

A Translation of
Fei Xiaotong's *Xiangtu Zhongguo*,
with an Introduction and Epilogue by
Gary G. Hamilton and Wang Zheng

University of California Press

Berkeley · Los Angeles · London

University of California Press
Berkeley and Los Angeles, California

University of California Press, Ltd.
London, England

© 1992 by
The Regents of the University of California

Library of Congress Cataloging-in-Publication Data
Fei, Hsiao-t'ung.
    [Hsiang t'u Chung-kuo. English]
    From the soil, the foundations of Chinese society : a
translation of Fei Xiaotong's Xiangtu Zhongguo, with an
introduction and epilogue / by Gary G. Hamilton and
Wang Zheng.
      p.   cm.
    Translation of: Hsiang t'u Chung-kuo.
    Includes index.
    ISBN 978-0-520-07796-6 (pbk. : alk. paper)
    1. China—Social conditions.   I. Hamilton, Gary G.
II. Wang, Zheng.   III. Title.
  HN733.5.F4513   1992
  306'.0951—dc20   91-28685
                             CIP

Printed in the United States of America

08 07 06

9 8 7

Contents

Foreword

The bulk of this book is a translation of *Xiangtu Zhongguo*, a set of essays written by Fei Xiaotong shortly after World War II. In writings about Fei and his works, the book's title is usually rendered in English as "rural China," but this rendering is inexact. *Xiang* means "countryside" and *tu* means "earth"; but the combination, *xiangtu*, is a set phrase meaning "one's native soil or home village." By using *xiangtu* to modify *Zhongguo* (China), Fei is conveying a subtle meaning to his readers: that Chinese society has grown out of its ties to the land. Should any of his readers miss the subtlety, Fei clarifies the meaning of the title in the book's first sentence, "Chinese society is fundamentally rural." "From the soil" captures Fei's meaning in a way that "rural China" does not.

Although this book is virtually unknown in the West, it is a standard text in many Chinese universities and contains ideas that are useful for Western readers as well. In our introduction, we explain why this book remains as fresh and as intellectually gripping today as it was over forty years ago, when it was first written. In fact, it may be even better suited to today's climate of opinion than to the earlier one, because Fei addresses the structural foundations of social pluralism and cultural diversity. By describing the fundamental differences between Chinese and Western societies, Fei helps us to understand the distinctiveness of Chinese society and to look at Western modernity in a new way.

We decided to translate this book because we were engaged in a similar pursuit. We, too, were contrasting China and the West in order to understand the distinctiveness of Chinese society; and on first reading Fei's book (Hamilton in 1985 and Wang in 1986), we were struck by the parallels between what we were trying to do and what Fei had already done forty years earlier. Moreover, once we had studied the book, it became increasingly evident that our subsequent work would have to build on Fei's insights. For this

vii

reason, we realized that we had to produce an English translation of the book and to explain how Fei's ideas open the way for understanding China and indeed other non-Western societies in new terms.

Throughout the book, Fei is attempting to explain to his Chinese readers what the West is like, so that he can show how Chinese society differs from Western societies. In our translation, we find ourselves having to cross the cultural barrier one additional time. Here we have had to convey in English what the West is like from a Chinese point of view, and to show how this Chinese understanding of the West allows the unique qualities of Chinese society to become visible to the very Chinese who would otherwise take those qualities for granted. Multiple levels of discourse needed to be included simultaneously. Throughout our translation, we have tried to emphasize Fei's Chinese point of view and to clarify this point of view for an English-reading public. As Fei himself has said, however, every act of translation is necessarily a new interpretation. We only hope that the English readers of this book will bracket their own taken-for-granted world—their Westernness—and allow themselves not only to enter a different social world but also to understand that that social world functions as fully as the world they themselves live in.

Xiangtu Zhongguo has been reissued many times in Taiwan and Hong Kong. For our translation, we used two reissued copies of the original edition.[1] One of the reissued editions was printed in Taiwan without publishing information or date of publication. The other edition was published in Hong Kong with publishing information but no date of publication.[2] Both editions were identical; we subsequently checked this version against a more recent edition published in Hong Kong.[3] With one exception, which we note in the text, this version is identical to the version we used in the translation.

For the epilogue, we also translated short passages from Fei's *Xiangtu chongjian* (Reconstructing rural China).[4] In the past, this

1. *Xiangtu Zhongguo* (Shanghai: Shanghai guanchashe, 1947).
2. *Xiangtu Zhongguo* (Xianggang: Wenxue chubanshe, n.d.).
3. *Xiangtu Zhongguo* (Xianggang: Sanlian shudian, 1986).
4. *Xiangtu chongjian* (Reconstructing rural China) (Shanghai: Shanghai guanchashe, 1948).

book has often been published in the same volume as *Xiangtu Zhongguo*, and both the Taiwan and Hong Kong volumes that we used to translate *Xiangtu Zhongguo* also contained the reissued 1948 edition of *Xiangtu chongjian*, which we used as the source of our translation.

We wish to acknowledge the assistance of a number of people and to express our thanks to them all. The students at the University of California, Davis, in a number of courses on complex organizations, comparative management, and Chinese societies, encouraged us by their enthusiastic reactions to our initial translations of chapters 4 and 5. Finding that people with no previous knowledge of China could enjoy and learn from these chapters prompted us to translate the entire book. The following people gave helpful comments on all or parts of this book (although we incorporated many of their suggestions, we are still responsible for the result): Tani Barlow, Eleanor Bender, Nicole Biggart, Thomas Gold, Lyn Lofland, Mausang Ng, Benjamin Orlove, Martha Winnacker, and especially Marco Orru, who also gave us the benefit of his editorial skills. We want to single out David Arkush for a special acknowledgment. His encouragement from the outset helped keep the project going, and his line-by-line reading of our translation saved us from many mistakes. Finally, we thank Sasha Bessom and Jean Stratford for assembling the manuscript and putting it into its present form.

G. G. H.
W. Z.

Introduction

Fei Xiaotong and the Beginnings of a Chinese Sociology

by Gary G. Hamilton and Wang Zheng

The book translated here, *Xiangtu Zhongguo,* began in the 1940s as lecture notes for an introductory class in Chinese rural society. The instructor of that class and the author of this book is Fei Xiaotong. The book that grew out of Fei's effort to introduce sociology to Chinese students is no ordinary textbook, and Fei is no ordinary sociologist.[1] He is the finest social scientist to emerge from China in the twentieth century, and *Xiangtu Zhongguo* is his chief theoretical statement about the nature of Chinese society. This is a book written by a Chinese for a Chinese audience about the distinctiveness of Chinese society. Because it presents an insider's view of a non-Western world, it is an unusual book for Westerners to read. But even at the time of its first publication in 1948, it was an unusual book for Chinese to read as well.

Fei rewrote and published his lecture notes chapter by chapter as a series of essays in a leading intellectual journal, *Shiji pinglun.* In the years immediately after World War II, before the Chinese revolution of 1949, Fei was already recognized as one of China's leading intellectuals and as a popular writer whose essays were widely read and admired. When Fei published the serialized version of *Xiangtu Zhongguo,* the essays immediately attracted attention; he quickly collected, revised, and published them in book

1. For the discussion of Fei's life, we have drawn extensively upon R. David Arkush's excellent biography, *Fei Xiaotong and Sociology in Revolutionary China* (Cambridge, Mass.: Harvard University Press, 1981), and Burton Pasternak's extensive interview with Fei, "A Conversation with Fei Xiaotong," *Current Anthropology* 29, no. 4 (Aug–Oct. 1988): 637–62. Also see James P. McGough's *Fei Hsiao-t'ung: The Dilemma of a Chinese Intellectual* (White Plains, N.Y.: M. E. Sharpe, 1979).

form in 1947. In the following year, he published a second book, *Xiangtu chongjian* (Reconstructing rural China)—another set of essays written over the same period and also published first in serialized form. The two books, often published together in the same volume, became Fei's most widely read works in Chinese. In the few years until 1952 (when the Communist government abolished the discipline of sociology on the mainland), these books made Fei famous among educated Chinese and one of the best-known advocates in China for reform.

The years between the end of World War II and the consolidation of Communist rule on the mainland mark a watershed in modern Chinese history. Fei's works barely survived the transition. After the Communist government banned sociology in 1952, it began to attack Fei and other sociologists who remained in the People's Republic of China as "rightist," bourgeois, and anti-Marxist.[2] *Xiangtu Zhongguo* and its companion volume, *Xiangtu chongjian*, went out of print and ceased to be readily available in the PRC. Across the Taiwan Straits, in Taiwan, where Chiang Kaishek and his Guomindang armies fled in 1949, writers who remained in Communist territory and expressed loyalty to the new government had their works officially restricted. Fei's writings existed in a gray zone, not readily available in bookstores and yet not totally unavailable. His books were sold in street stalls without his name or with his name shortened to Fei Tong, and universities were not allowed to include them in officially approved reading lists.[3] Therefore, beginning in the 1950s, aside from a continuing readership in Hong Kong, the books that Fei had written in Chinese were not readily available and were no longer studied as closely as they had been before the political climate changed. Ironically, in the same years, Fei's books in English were widely read and became quite influential.[4]

Since the late 1970s, the situation has changed. On the mainland, beginning with reforms after Mao Zedong's death in 1976,

2. See McGough, *Fei Hsiao-t'ung*, for a discussion of these attacks and some translations of the most influential criticisms.

3. For a listing of the various editions of *Xiangtu Zhongguo* before 1980, see Arkush, *Fei Xiaotong*, p. 332.

4. See note 7 below.

Fei and other intellectuals labeled earlier as rightists were gradually rehabilitated. In 1979, sociology was reinstated as an academic discipline; and the Chinese Society of Sociology was founded, with Fei as its first president. However, Fei's pre-1949 writings were not immediately reissued.[5] Fei even had to use mimeographed versions of *Xiangtu Zhongguo* and *Xiangtu chongjian* in his course when he began offering graduate training to a small group of students at Beijing University in the early 1980s. Although Fei Xiaotong is once again a widely known figure and although some of his pre-1949 writings, including *Xiangtu Zhongguo*, are now available in the PRC, these writings have only recently become known outside of a small group of sociologists.[6]

In Chinese-speaking areas outside the PRC, *Xiangtu Zhongguo* is today regarded as a classic text that lays a foundation for understanding Chinese society in its own terms. In Hong Kong, most of Fei's works, including *Xiangtu Zhongguo*, were reissued after 1980, and *Xiangtu Zhongguo* began to serve as a standard text for understanding Chinese society. In Taiwan, where Fei's works are still not officially approved, many of Fei's pre-1949 books, with full attribution to his authorship, became readily available in market bookstalls even before the new Hong Kong editions appeared. In Taiwan, too, the ideas from *Xiangtu Zhongguo* became part of the established wisdom about how to interpret Chinese society. In the

5. *Xiangtu Zhongguo* became available only in 1986, when the Hong Kong edition, published by Sanlian Press, appeared. Since 1986, several volumes of Fei's selected works have been published in the PRC, including *Fei Xiaotong xuanji* (Selected works of Fei Xiaotong) (Tianjin: Renmin Publishing Co., 1988) and *Fei Xiaotong xueshu jinghua lu* (The best academic writings of Fei Xiaotong) (Beijing: Normal University Press, 1988). Both contain selected chapters from *Xiangtu Zhongguo*.

6. Fei is better known in China today for his political than for his intellectual roles. When he was rehabilitated after the Cultural Revolution, he became a well-known political figure. In 1989, he was vice president of the National People's Congress and president of the Democratic League of China. He is regarded as one of the leading figures in the democratic political movements, a role he had already played during World War II. In the post-1978 period in the PRC, the Democratic League is, in principle, supposed to consult with Community Party leaders on policy issues—although, in fact, its role, as well as that of its leaders, seems largely honorific. Drawing upon his small-town research, Fei does appear to have had some influence on the development of economic reforms after 1978. For a survey of this research, see Fei's recent book *Small Towns in China* (Beijing: New World Press, 1986). For more on Fei's activities in the early years of the Democratic League, see Arkush, *Fei Xiaotong*, pp. 178ff.

English-speaking world, however, although Fei Xiaotong is the best-known Chinese social scientist, *Xiangtu Zhongguo* is virtually unknown.[7]

THE MAKING OF A
CHINESE SOCIOLOGIST

Xiangtu Zhongguo represents Fei Xiaotong's first and only effort to construct a non-Western theoretical foundation for a sociology of Chinese society. Only a few years after *Xiangtu Zhongguo* appeared in print, Marxist social analysis became intellectual orthodoxy throughout China. All attempts to develop ideas that would run counter to this orthodoxy were forbidden, and transgressors were severely punished.[8] As we will discuss later in the introduction and again in the epilogue, Fei's sociology of Chinese society runs directly counter to a Chinese Marxist interpretation of Chinese society. It offers a very different view of the society and recommends a very different course of action for facing China's economic and social problems. Consequently, it has not had a chance for a full hearing in the People's Republic of China. But even without the hearing in the PRC, Fei's pre-1949 writings and their theoretical centerpiece, *Xiangtu Zhongguo*, are now regarded as well-grounded and challenging attempts to develop a sociology of Chinese society.[9] In fact, Fei's *Xiangtu Zhongguo* represents one of the few and certainly one of the most insightful efforts to build a sociology of a non-Western society.

Fei, the son of a schoolteacher and the youngest of five children,

7. Fei is best known in the West for a series of books and articles published in English between 1939 and early the 1950s. See, especially, *Peasant Life in China* (London: Routledge and Kegan Paul, 1939); *Earthbound China*, written with Zhang Ziyi (Chicago: University of Chicago Press, 1945); "Peasantry and Gentry: An Interpretation of Chinese Social Structure and Its Changes," *American Journal of Sociology* 52 (1946): 1–17; and *China's Gentry* (Chicago: University of Chicago Press, 1953). Some of Fei's post-1949 works have been translated in McGough's *Fei Hsiao-t'ung* and, most recently, in Fei's *Rural Development in China: Prospect and Retrospect* (Chicago: University of Chicago Press, 1989). For Fei's bibliography to 1980, see Arkush, *Fei Xiaotong*.

8. See Fei's discussion in Pasternak, "A Conversation with Fei Xiaotong."

9. Another very significant and more recent effort to create a "sinified" sociology has occurred in Taiwan. See, in particular, Kuo-shu Yang and Chung-I Wen (eds.), *Shehui ji xingwei kexue yanjiu de Zhongguo hua* (The sinicization of social and behavioral science research in China), Monograph Series B, no. 10 (Taipei: Institute of Ethnology, Academia Sinica, 1982).

was born in the central Chinese province of Jiangsu in 1910. Following the lead of his older siblings, Fei attended local missionary schools and eventually entered the missionary-sponsored Soochow University. An honors student, Fei began preparing for a medical degree, but he switched to sociology after transferring, as a junior, to another missionary school, Yanjing University in Beijing. Fifty years later, talking about his decision to change his major from medicine to sociology, Fei said, "My reasoning was that as a medical doctor I might cure the afflictions of a few, but not those of hundreds of millions engendered by an irrational society. What ails society must be cured first. . . . To be a doctor we have to learn physiology first; likewise, to cure the society we have to study social theories first." [10] With the practical goal of understanding Chinese society in order to change it, Fei started his long journey toward establishing a sociology of China.

Although Fei Xiaotong was primarily concerned with Chinese social problems, his training was mainly Western. At Yanjing University, he worked with American-trained teachers, and in the fall of his senior year, in 1932, he studied with the American sociologist Robert Park. Teaching in China for one term, Park had recently retired from the chair of the department of sociology at the University of Chicago, then the best-known sociology department in the world. Park had a great influence on that department and played a central role in creating what had become known as the Chicago school of sociology. [11] He was a well-known critic of ivory-tower theorizing and an outspoken advocate for a sociology based on field research. A dynamic teacher, Park preached that message to Fei, who thereafter turned decisively from library research and reading about Western theories to actual observation of Chinese society.

Entering graduate school and now attracted to field research, Fei

10. See Fei Xiaotong, *Toward a People's Anthropology* (Beijing: New World Press, 1981), p. i; and *Congshi shehuixue wushi nian* (Fifty years in sociology) (Tianjin: People's Press, n.d.), p. 2. We might note that modern China's great author, Lu Xun, and modern China's first renowned revolutionary, Sun Yat-sen, both gave up medicine for the same reasons.

11. For a discussion of the Chicago school of sociology and of Park's role in that school, see Fred H. Matthews, *Quest of an American Sociology: Robert E. Park and the Chicago School* (Montreal: McGill-Queen's University Press, 1977), and Martin Bulmer, *The Chicago School of Sociology* (Chicago: University of Chicago Press, 1984).

switched focus once again from sociology, which in China was a more library-oriented discipline, to anthropology. Fei took his graduate training with the Russian anthropologist S. M. Shirokogoroff at Qinghua University. Shirokogoroff was devoted to the empirical study of the social organization and physical characteristics of tribal peoples in China, and under his direction Fei enhanced his appreciation of empirical research and developed a life-long interest in studying China's minorities. After receiving his master's degree, Fei won a British Boxer Indemnity Fund scholarship and, in the fall of 1936, attended the London School of Economics and Political Science, where he studied anthropology under Bronislaw Malinowski.

In the 1930s, Malinowski, then in his early fifties, was the world's preeminent social anthropologist.[12] He was a pioneer of anthropological techniques of field research and of the type of theorizing that emerged from intensive fieldwork. His field research among the Trobriand Islanders, published in a series of books, had established the theoretical and methodological standards for anthropology in his day. Under his leadership, the discipline of anthropology was transformed. Instead of taking a distant, comparative, evolutionary approach to "primitive" peoples, anthropologists now attempted to understand tribal societies in terms of their own worldviews. One of Malinowski's principal ideas, and one that Fei took back to China with him, was that valid social theories are those that account for reality as perceived and created by social actors themselves. Malinowski worked closely with Fei, and they developed what Fei's biographer, David Arkush, called a "warm avuncular relationship."[13] Fei received his Ph.D. in two years. In 1945, Fei paid homage to "my three esteemed masters, Professors S. M. Shirokogoroff, R. E. Park, and B. Malinowski. From them I inherited most of my ideas."[14]

Fei was attracted to Western social scientists who told him that the best theories are those that emerge from an intimate, systematic knowledge of the society being studied. These Western schol-

12. For a summary of Malinowski's life and works, see Adam Kuper, *Anthropologists and Anthropology: The British School, 1922–1972* (New York: Pica Press, 1973).
13. Arkush, *Fei Xiaotong*, p. 43.
14. *Earthbound China*, p. xiv; "Studying in England," in *Revisiting England* (Hunan: People's Press, 1983), pp. 174–85; Arkush, *Fei Xiaotong*, p. 24.

ars told Fei, in essence, that adequate theories of China must be based on intensive, firsthand knowledge of Chinese society itself. In Fei's time, and even today, however, many theories applied to China were first developed in studies of the West. Most standard theories about the nature of economic development, religious movements, political structure, social organization, and even human emotions have been derived from observations made in Western societies. Conducting such investigations, many scholars abstract the basic conclusions of their studies and offer them as theories for further testing. The assumption is that researchers need to search for general theories, theories that apply in varying degrees to all societies and to all people, regardless of time and place. This type of theorizing does not require that all societies or all individuals be identical. Rather, theories themselves become a sort of model against which societies and individuals can be compared. When applied to a particular setting, the model more or less fits; and the analyst then reaches a conclusion about how, in that particular context, societies work and individuals act. The model becomes the standard; sociological knowledge becomes a probabilistic assessment of how well the real world conforms to the predictions of the model.

Park, Malinowski, and later Fei took a strong stand against this type of theorizing. In one form or another, they all argued that valid social knowledge cannot be obtained through testing deductive models in different social contexts. The goal of social science is not to discover what is similar in all societies. At this level, such similarities turn out to be superficial and actually limit, even undermine, the understanding of why people act as they do. For instance, as Fei points out in *Xiangtu Zhongguo*, that people in all societies create something we can call a "family" says very little about the complexity and variations in what actually constitutes a family. What is important to discover, then, are differences among people and among societies; these differences are what cause societies to change in distinctive ways.

The first step in understanding differences is to understand how people in any one context actually conduct their lives. This approach calls for intensive research into a specific social context, rather than an extensive application of a theory across many contexts. Out of this intensive understanding, the researcher develops sensitizing concepts, or what Fei, drawing on Max Weber's sociology, calls "ideal types."[15] Ideal types synthesize and somewhat exaggerate actual patterns of behavior, and in turn can be used both to analyze actual behavior within that society and to contrast similar but ultimately different patterns of behavior in other societies.

This is the methodology that Fei employs in *Xiangtu Zhongguo*, but he began to develop this methodology very early in his quest to understand Chinese society. It is illustrated in his first major research project, a study carried out in the aftermath of a tragic accident that took the life of his wife and left Fei badly injured.[16] The accident occurred in 1935, when Fei and his wife of less than five months were conducting a survey among Yao tribes in remote regions of Guangxi province. Fei was caught in a "dead fall" tiger trap, and his wife, running for help, drowned when crossing a river. After the accident, Fei returned to his hometown in Jiangsu province to recuperate. While staying with his sister in the village of Kaixiangong, Fei started an ethnography of the village, in which he tried to understand rural life in the same terms that the peasants understood it. In the summer of 1936, he collected material on the village's economic system and social structure and took his notes with him when he went to England to study with Malinowski in the fall of that year. Later, under Malinowski's direction, he used these materials to write his renowned book *Peasant Life in China*.

The publication of *Peasant Life in China* in 1939 made Fei an avantgarde intellectual among the non-Marxist sociologists in China. In the late 1920s and early 1930s, universities across China had started sociology departments, and sociology had become one of the most popular majors. Western academic sociology quickly became influential among other intellectuals as well. However, during this pioneering period, many well-known works produced by Chinese sociologists were rudimentary social surveys and were often aimed

15. In his foreword to the 1986 reissue of *Xiangtu Zhongguo*, Fei characterizes his ideal-typical methodology as follows: "My attempt to abstract concepts from concrete phenomena in order to understand the phenomena better is similar to the use of what are called ideal types in English. Ideal types belong to the realm of reason. They are neither fictitious nor ideal; rather, they are concepts formed as part of a cognitive process and are used to synthesize something that is general, so that it can be applied to concrete situations. Since a concept is formed through abstracting from concrete situations, it has to be continuously tested in concrete situations in order to reduce error" (pp. ii–iii).

16. For an account of the accident, see Arkush, *Fei Xiaotong*, pp. 60–69.

at correcting social problems. When it appeared, Fei's *Peasant Life in China* was an extraordinary work. It was a description of life as it was actually lived, rather than a recipe for social change. Throughout the book, reflecting Malinowski's theory of social functionalism, Fei tried to demonstrate the interrelationships among various aspects of life in a rural village. This sophisticated effort attracted the attention of Western scholars and marked Fei's first step toward understanding rural Chinese society.[17]

When Fei returned to China from England in the fall of 1938, the northern and coastal cities had been occupied by Japan. Fei went to Kunming, the capital city of Yunnan province in extreme southwestern China, which was to become the wartime intellectual center of Free China. There he obtained a position in the sociology department at Yunnan University and by 1941 was promoted to full professor and head of the department. At the same time, he and his close colleagues conducted field research coordinated through the Yanjing-Yunnan Station for Sociological Research. In 1940, Fei became the field director as well.

The decade 1938–1948 was the most effervescent period of Chinese sociology.[18] During this period, Fei finished his second village ethnography, *Paddy Fields of Lucun*. More significantly, he became the head of a team of young researchers who, under his direction, consciously and brilliantly strove to create a Chinese sociology. The team of about ten people produced a dozen monographs, all based on field research in the area, bearing such titles as Zhang Ziyi's *Land and Capital in Yicun*, Tian Rukang's *Female Workers in a Cotton Mill*, Li Yuyi's *Economics of a Mixed Community of Lolos and Chinese*, Gu Bao's *The Power Structure in a Rural Community in Yunnan*, and Francis Hsu's *Magic and Science in Western Yunnan: A Study of the Introduction of Modern Medicine in a Rustic Community*.[19] Fei translated some of these works into English and

17. Lucie Cheng and Alvin So, "The Reestablishment of Sociology in the PRC," *Annual Review of Sociology* 9 (1983): 471–98.

18. Arkush, *Fei Xiaotong*, p. 100.

19. For a complete list of these works and some description of the team effort behind the research monographs, see Fei's introduction to *Earthbound China*. Also see Wilma Fairbank, *America's Cultural Experiment in China, 1942–1949*, Department of State Publication 8839 (Washington, D.C.: U.S. Government Printing Office, 1976), pp. 96–97, for a brief description of the Yanjing Yunnan field station with Fei in charge.

had them published.[20] Largely through Fei's efforts, these studies attracted so much international attention that the eminent social anthropologist Maurice Freedman concluded, "It could be argued that before the Second World War, outside North America and Western Europe, China was the seat of the most flourishing sociology in the world, at least in respect to its intellectual quality."[21]

Fei devoted more time to writing and lecturing than to field research in the immediate postwar period. Knowing that great changes would occur in the coming years, Fei wrote prolifically, publishing numerous essays in newspapers and periodicals and quickly becoming a well-known writer. While popularizing sociological ideas and commenting on political issues of the time, he was also engaged in what he called "the second phase" of a sociology of China, the work of conceptualizing Chinese social structure.[22] *Xiangtu Zhongguo* was by far the most important theoretical work of this phase. Therein, Fei develops a comparative, historical approach to depicting the characteristics of Chinese society, and his aim is clearly to provide a theoretical framework for the study of this society.

Although Fei had hoped to contribute something theoretically more substantial and better documented than *Xiangtu Zhongguo*, he was not to have the opportunity. When the Communists took over China in 1949, Fei decided to stay in China and sincerely supported the new government. Although he had not been close to the Communists, Mao's peasant revolution aroused Fei's sympathy because he, like Mao, was deeply concerned with rural problems. Fei believed that the new China needed sociology, and he hoped to develop a Chinese sociology in the process of building a new China. As a prominent scholar, he was treated well by the Communist leaders in the early 1950s, when they were eager to gain the support of intellectuals.

The discipline of sociology, however, was soon abolished. By 1952, under increasing Russian influence, Chinese party leaders adopted a more dogmatic attitude: Marxism-Leninism was the only true social science, and sociology was merely a bourgeois pseudo-

---

20. The two translations still available are *Earthbound China* and Kuo-heng Shih's *China Enters the Machine Age*, trans. Fei Xiaotong and Francis L. K. Hsu (Cambridge, Mass.: Harvard University Press, 1944).

21. Quoted in Arkush, *Fei Xiaotong*, p. 94.

22. "Postscript," *Xiangtu Zhongguo* (1986 ed.), p. 89.

science. With the abrupt dismissal of sociology, Fei and some other sociologists were transferred to work on the "problems" of the national minorities, a field of investigation that was less controversial and about which policymakers needed information. But even there, Fei had to incorporate Marxist historical theories and the concepts of class struggle into his ethnological research.[23]

Fei's hope of restoring sociology was rekindled in the Hundred Flowers period, between 1956 and 1957, when Mao proposed the slogan "Let a hundred flowers bloom, let a hundred schools of thought contend."[24] Fei and other sociologists started to discuss the formation of a Chinese sociological association and the restoration of sociology departments. To continue his own sociological research, Fei revisited Kaixiangong, hoping to observe changes in the village he had studied twenty years before. But before he could finish his research project, the political atmosphere suddenly changed. Now Mao felt that free discussions and criticism by intellectuals threatened the authority of the Communist Party. These bourgeois intellectuals had to be contained by a proletarian dictatorship. Fei, as one of the prominent scholars in China, was criticized publicly for his "conspiracy" in restoring bourgeois sociology and was labeled a "rightist."[25] From the 1957 Antirightist Movement to the end of the Cultural Revolution, Fei was forced to abandon his academic work and was removed from high positions.[26] During a period of the Cultural Revolution, as Fei later reported in an interview, he "was responsible for [cleaning] all the toilets in one building."[27]

In 1978, the new party leaders advocated rapid modernization as a way to improve Chinese economic and social conditions. The value of intellectuals was once again recognized, and both natural and social sciences were promoted. Against this background, Fei

23. Pasternak, "A Conversation with Fei Xiaotong," p. 650; Arkush, *Fei Xiaotong*, p. 228.
24. McGough (in *Fei Hsiao-t'ung*, pp. 32–38) translates Fei's hopes that sociology would be reinstated as an academic discipline.
25. See McGough, *Fei Hsiao-t'ung*, pp. 75–151, for translations of some of the most stinging published criticisms of Fei, as well as Fei's own "confession." See Pasternak, "A Conversation with Fei Xiaotong," for Fei's recollection of this period.
26. Recalling those years, Fei said that he had lost twenty years: "It was intellectual stagnation." See Pasternak, "A Conversation with Fei Xiaotong,'" pp. 547–651.
27. Ibid., p. 652.

Xiaotong returned to national prominence, and sociology was restored as an academic discipline. Since early 1979, when Fei became the first president of the Chinese Society of Sociology, he again devoted himself to establishing a Chinese sociology. In contrast to his stance thirty years earlier, however, he now more cautiously advocated a Chinese sociology developed under the guidance of Marxism.[28] In his recently published works, Fei often mentions the great example of Mao, a person who successfully applied Marxism to Chinese reality and who emphasized the importance of social investigation.[29] According to a former graduate student, however, in the course Fei taught to his graduate students in the early 1980s, he required three texts, all by himself and all written before 1949: *Shengyu zhidu* (Systems of reproduction); *Xiangtu chongjian*; and the book we have translated here, *Xiangtu Zhongguo*.

READING THE TEXT

In 1986, Fei Xiaotong characterized his writing of *Xiangtu Zhongguo* as an exploratory journey undertaken in his youth, a journey to discover and describe, in bold and simple strokes, a sociology of Chinese society.[30] Such a sociology should not mindlessly import concepts and theories from Western learning. Well trained in Western theories and widely traveled in the Occident, Fei recognized that Western concepts did not work well in the analysis of

28. In recent years, Fei's reputation for being overcautious has grown. He has been accused of being a spokesman for the current regime and of not speaking forcefully for human rights and for those involved in the "democracy movement" in 1989. The accuracy of these accusations will not be known until more is learned about the factional disputes that have occurred within the ruling elite since 1978.

29. For instance, in a chapter entitled in English "The Attempt to Do Ethnosociological Surveys" (*Congshi shehuixue wushi nian*, pp. 83–84), Fei writes that social investigation "is a well-developed tradition in the [Communist] party that Chairman Mao repeatedly advocated. Is it not Chairman Mao's great contribution that he introduced Marxism and Leninism to China and that he created Mao Zedong thought by applying Marxism and Leninism to Chinese reality? Chairman Mao sought truth from facts. By investigating and studying the Chinese situation, he expanded Marxism. . . . Although Mao Zedong's thought has grown out of Marxism, we should not regard this as an end. We should continue to develop [social theory]. How can we do this? Daydreaming will not accomplish this. We have to go out into reality and truthfully observe the changes in China."

30. Fei Xiaotong, "Jiuzhu 'Xiangtu Zhongguo' chongkan xuyan" (Foreword to the reissue of *Xiangtu Zhongguo*) (Xianggang: Sanlian shudian, 1986), p. i.

Chinese society. Instead, he wanted to fashion concepts for the locale, concepts that would synthesize a lived-in reality and make that reality understandable to all. His was not a chauvinistic response but a genuine intellectual assessment. *Xiangtu Zhongguo* is a sustained effort to break through all the conceptual clutter that surrounded attempts to understand China and to lay out, all at once and in the simplest possible way, a theoretical framework and some key concepts for the study of Chinese society.

The resulting work is surprisingly straightforward, so much so that the book's very simplicity masks the brilliance of theory that Fei is trying to communicate. Because the book is so simply written, the complexity and significance of the thesis are not fully appreciated on a first reading. Misunderstanding is easy because the text can be read at three different levels: as a literary essay, as a sociology of China, and as a political document. Each reading gives a somewhat different message.

THE LITERARY ESSAY

Xiangtu Zhongguo was published as a series of essays written for a literate audience, the urban, educated minority. Although the original ideas came from lecture notes for Fei's course in introductory rural sociology, by the time they appeared in *Xiangtu Zhongguo*, they had been stripped of most of their academic qualities. Fei wrote the essays in a plain style—stark, with almost no footnotes or scholarly pretensions, and with vivid examples from daily life. In this book, as well as in most of his subsequent writings, Fei adopted a style of presentation quite distinct from the quasi-classical writing preferred by most essayists.[31] His style of writing downplayed his learning. In fact, the book is almost conversational in tone and was obviously written to be accessible to the largest possible audience,

31. Fei acknowledges this style of writing in the introduction to his collected works. He describes himself as being "strong at short essays and weak at long works. . . . Even with *Shengyu zhidu* [Systems of reproduction] and *Xiangtu Zhongguo*, the books that needed a large space to express my ideas clearly, I still divided them into short essays with many subtitles. The short essays were produced one after another, somewhat similar to a television series." Fei says that he writes his essays "with one breath," that in his youth he would "never let [his] articles remain unfinished overnight" (Foreword, *Fei Xiaotong xueshu jinghua lu*, pp. 3–4). *Shengyu zhidu* was published in Shanghai in 1947.

to be widely read, and to be quickly understood. In our translation, we have tried to convey the simplicity of the prose.

Fei's prose style is disarming. Fei, in fact, called himself a "fast hand" *(kuaishou)*, a quick writer, saying that he knew that "fast does not necessarily mean good."[32] He also expressed doubts that this style of writing "would be accepted into the temple of academe" because he does not quote the classics much, does not use statistics, and never writes prose filled with obscure terminology or jargon.[33] This form of exposition makes Fei's ideas seem at times too simple, too straightforward, and too matter-of-fact. Fei usually does not acknowledge the nuances in his theories and does not follow their logical implications; moreover, Fei does not tell his readers the source of his ideas. There are only vague references to an occasional Western thinker: He mentions Emile Durkheim in one passage and refers to the social realist school in American legal theory; but none of the connections is brought out, and only someone trained in the West could catch many of them. The ideas themselves, however, are quite sophisticated and indicate that Fei actively followed and reacted to developments in Western sociological theory. In particular, he shows his interest in American pragmatism, a philosophy that influenced the Chicago school of sociology. Chapters 2 and 3 of *Xiangtu Zhongguo*, where Fei introduces his readers to his basic sociological perspective, are devoted to expositions of ideas associated with George Herbert Mead and with what is now called symbolic interactionism. Later in the book, he acknowledges his debt to the pragmatist philosopher William James. Still, much of the clear-minded theorizing that went into this book is hidden by the simplicity of his essay format.

By serializing his essays in a popular journal, Fei hoped to reach an audience who would not be impressed with a demonstration of erudition or with a pedantic style. Instead, he was writing to the educated intellectuals in 1947, the people who would be trying to resolve the massive political, social, and economic problems the country was facing at the time. With *Xiangtu Zhongguo*, Fei was trying to persuade the intellectual elite and win them over to his vision—that China was *obviously* founded on certain structural

32. *Fei Xiaotong xueshu jinghua lu*, pp. 3–4.
33. Ibid.

principles and that those principles needed to be respected in any attempt at social change. *Xiangtu Zhongguo* was written as if Fei were sitting in the same room with the future leaders of China and telling them in plain, simple language that Chinese society could be saved if only they recognized the obvious—those principles of society that every Chinese knew intimately and instinctively. All Chinese, including the elite, lived by these principles but did not recognize them, because they had been nowhere else and had known nothing different. Because China's future was at hand, the effort of persuasion required the simplest of styles.

THE SOCIOLOGY OF CHINESE SOCIETY

Fei's desire to persuade China's intellectuals derived from his own understanding of Chinese society and of how to change it. His understanding of China developed out of his larger effort to formulate the basic principles of Chinese society. Such an effort was needed, he believed, because most of the social science then taught in China was directly imported from the West and had little relevance to China. Fei recalled his own education in China: "Courses taught by Americans or American-trained Chinese were naturally more apt to deal with American labor legislation that with Chinese villages."[34] Fei disliked this situation. "Those courses rarely touched Chinese society. After taking them, I still did not understand what Chinese society was and why there were so many problems here. I was unlikely to find ready answers from the textbooks. So [our team of sociologists] decided to observe, investigate, analyze, and study our own society. That is to say we wanted to establish a Chinese sociology."[35] It was Fei's conviction that "Western innovations are never precisely appropriate; we need to Sinicize them."[36] Therefore, starting with a clear understanding of Western theory, Fei and his colleagues began their fieldwork and gradually and systematically learned about Chinese society.

Xiangtu Zhongguo embodies the lessons learned from systematic observation and careful comparisons, but the book contains few comments about Fei's field research itself. To convey his theories

34. Arkush, *Fei Xiaotong*, pp. 27–28.
35. *Congshi shehuixue wushi nian*, p. 2.
36. Pasternak, "A Conversation with Fei Xiaotong," p. 659.

about Chinese society, Fei uses two levels of comparison. The first level is an urban-rural comparison. This level of comparison in the book is actually a rhetorical device. In China, there was (and is today) a large gap between the style of life of the rural population and that of the people who live in China's cosmopolitan urban areas. Fei's audience consisted mainly of urbanites. In fact, the periodical in which Fei published *Xiangtu Zhongguo* was located in Shanghai, the most cosmopolitan city in Asia during the first half of the twentieth century, and its readership was largely from Shanghai. Fei used the rural-urban comparison as a device to get his urban, literate readers to understand their rural origins. The comparison is implicitly one of similarity, and the message is that patterns in rural society provide the foundation for all of Chinese society.

The rural-urban contrast is blurred when Fei uses the urban half of the dichotomy to stand for a China that is changing. In this context, he sees urban China either as a corruption of Chinese patterns or as an attempt to leave what is intrinsically Chinese and to move, somewhat artificially, toward a different, essentially modern, Westernized society. This typification of urban society even further emphasizes that rural China is a metaphor for all of Chinese society.

The second level of comparison is a contrast between China and the West. As we will explain in the next section, this contrast forms the theoretical core of the book. Through such contrast, Fei seeks to unveil the distinctive qualities of Chinese society. He reveals to his readers the world they know well but take for granted, and he sets that known reality against Western reality. His message is that, for reasons easily explained, Chinese social patterns differ from those found elsewhere. There are, accordingly, no universal social patterns and no universally valid principles by which all societies are held together. Western theories and Western solutions to social problems, therefore, cannot be automatically applied to China. Instead, those who seek to change China must first understand the distinctive qualities of Chinese society.

By creating a sociology *of* China, Fei hoped to create a sociology *for* China. He wanted to show others the principles on which Chinese society is based and to demonstrate how such a society might be changed for the better. *Xiangtu Zhongguo* describes the principles, and *Xiangtu chongjian* describes China's social problems and the ways to go about solving them. In the next section, we outline the most important of these principles. In our epilogue, we show how Fei applied these principles in recommending solutions to China's social problems.

The Political Document

Although *Xiangtu Zhongguo* is a text outlining a theory of Chinese society, it must also be read as a political document. In this role, *Xiangtu Zhongguo* and *Xiangtu chongjian* are indeed companion pieces. The first presents the theory, the second the application; together, they form an agenda for political action.

Fei wrote both sets of essays quickly and back to back. He wrote them simply, so that they would be easily read and understood, and he published them at a time when their effect on the political process would be the greatest. In 1947, the path that China would take was anyone's guess, but it was clear that great changes lay immediately ahead. Fei took the responsibility, which intellectuals in China often took, to argue for a particular course of action, a course of action guided by his sociological understanding of China. "History," wrote Fei in 1947, "is not always rational, but any historical circumstance contains a rational way. Whether history can develop rationally depends on whether people can behave rationally. As a person regarded as a scholar, I have the responsibility to point out the rational direction. Whether this recommendation can be turned into history, that is a matter for politicians."[37]

In *Xiangtu Zhongguo*, Fei used his sociology as a platform for a political agenda. It was a role sociology had played before. In the United States, between 1890 and 1920, the social sciences, including sociology, had a crucial role in leading the reform movements that shaped modern American society. Knowing about this role, and sensing the transformative impact that sociology could have in conceptualizing the change in Chinese society, Fei used his sociology as a way to envision and to argue for China's future. The road that Fei wanted China to take was the road of gradual change, a change that would build upon the strengths of Chinese society,

37. "Postscript," *Xiangtu Zhongguo*, p. 88.

making them the foundation for China's modernization. The implicit message was simple enough: China is rapidly changing and everything is in flux. Change, however, must be clearly understood in terms of what is actually occurring in Chinese society. China is not the West, and so what evolved in the West should not be seen as evidence of a universal pattern or as a recipe for China to follow blindly. Instead, China has its own destiny, its own path, and that path is surely shaped by the patterns internal to Chinese society. Fei undoubtedly hoped that the new leaders coming into power would understand this message and would adopt his suggestions.

A part of Fei's message is an implicit criticism of alien theories applied to China. At several points in *Xiangtu Zhongguo*, Fei states clearly that Western theories do not adequately conceptualize Chinese society. Fei does not mention Marxist analysis by name, although he clearly alludes to it in his discussion of the conflict perspective in Chapter 10 of *Xiangtu Zhongguo*. It is not difficult to see there that Fei's sociology and a Marxist interpretation of Chinese society are at odds. Although Mao Zedong provided an indigenous version of Marxism, Mao's Marxism and Fei's sociology still worked in opposite directions and aimed at different goals. Simply stated, Mao wanted to eradicate the old society and create an entirely new social order; he was the quintessential revolutionary. In contrast, Fei wanted to retain many elements of the old society and use those elements as the foundation on which to build a modernized society; Fei was the quintessential reformist. For this reason, if for no other, Fei's sociology waned as Mao's Marxism dominated the first thirty years of the People's Republic of China.

FEI'S THEORY OF CHINESE SOCIETY

Some readers may prefer to read this section after they read the text, and therefore discover, without any prompting from us, the significance of Fei's theory of Chinese society. Others, particularly those less familiar either with Chinese society or with general sociological theory, may find this introduction to Fei's theory useful in understanding Fei's insights. In the footnotes to this section, we provide references to the work of other sociologists who have made use of Fei's concepts and theories.

In *Xiangtu Zhongguo*, Fei integrates all levels of analysis, from social psychology to social structure, in an attempt to give a comprehensive view of Chinese society. Fei does not describe concrete social patterns as he did in his earlier ethnographies. Instead, he builds his sociology on the development of models or ideal types, and he sharpens these models through contrasts with models drawn from other societies. "First," says Fei, "we should start with our own society, and then we may study others for purposes of comparison. I am an outsider to [the United States], but I can see how different it is from mine through such comparisons. We can compare models."[38]

CHAXUGEJU

The main theory that Fei develops analytically to describe Chinese society depicts the principles of Chinese social organization. Fei's core thesis is that Chinese society is organized through principles different from those prevailing in the West. Organizational principles are to a society what a grammar is to a language. The principles provide the structural framework for social action; they are intuitive and taken for granted; they are deeply embedded in people's worldviews, as well as in the society that people re-create every day.

Fei introduces Chinese organizational principles through the concept of *chaxugeju*.[39] We have translated *chaxugeju* as "differential mode of association," but the term is awkward in Chinese and is difficult to translate. *Cha* means "difference" or "dissimilarity," *xu* means "order" or "sequence," and *geju* means "pattern" or "framework." As Fei develops the concept in chapters 4 and 5, it is clear that he uses the term to describe analytically the patterning of Chinese society through nonequivalent, ranked categories of social relationships *(shehui guanxi)*. This concept is very complex, and

38. Pasternak, "A Conversation with Fei Xiaotong," p. 660.
39. The English pronunciation of this word is "cha-shoe-ge-jew." Ichiro Numazaki first suggested to us that *chaxugeju* be translated as "differential mode of association." We should note that in J. Mason Gentzler's translation of chapter 4 of *Xiangtu Zhongguo (Changing China* [New York: Praeger, 1977], pp. 210–14), *chaxugeju* was left untranslated, because Gentzler said that no suitable translation could be found.

behind it lies a comprehensive theory of Chinese society. The concept allows us entry into that theory.

By using a term that is awkward in Chinese, Fei is trying to get his Chinese readers to recognize a distinctive characteristic of their own society—namely, that Chinese society consists of a meticulous ranking of people, who are classified according to distinct categories of social relationship. Because Chinese readers would intuitively recognize this fact and think it obvious and unimportant, Fei introduces the concept of *chaxugeju* and contrasts it to a model of Western social organization.

Fei uses two extended metaphors to convey the contrast forcefully to his readers. Western society is represented by straws collected to form a haystack, and Chinese society is represented by the ripples flowing out from the splash of a rock thrown into water. These two metaphors share no common ground, so implicitly Fei asks his readers to think of the two societies as being organized in completely different ways. He says, in effect, that Chinese society cannot be adequately conceptualized in terms of haystacks (i.e., organizations) nor the West in terms of ripples in water (i.e., discrete categories of social relationships).

Through these metaphors, he argues that in the West individuals produce their society by applying an "organizational mode of association" *(tuantigeju)*. People create groups that have clear boundaries. Membership in these groups is unambiguous; everyone knows who is and who is not a member. And the rights and duties of members are clearly delineated. Such groups are organizations, and they, in turn, shape Western society's social structure. These organizations are the firms in the economy, the bureaucracies in the government, the universities in the educational system, and the clubs in local society. They are everywhere and serve as devices for framing individualism in modern Western societies. By contrast, people in China create their society by applying another logic, the logic of *chaxugeju*, the "differential mode of association." With this mode of association, the society is composed not of discrete organizations but of overlapping networks of people linked together through differentially categorized social relationships. These networks have four key features.

First, networks are discontinuous. They do not link people together in a single systematic way; rather, networks center on the individual and have a different composition for each person. Because each person is at the center of his or her own network, Fei calls Chinese society "egocentric," and he shows the substantial differences in logic between an ego-centered Chinese society and an individualistic Western society. The Western mode of association presupposes the autonomy of individuals, whereas the Chinese mode of association presupposes multiple linkages of self with others and a categorization of those linkages. Fei attempts to explain the origins of both modes of association through an undeveloped historical and cultural argument.[40] He traces the Western organizational mode of association to Christianity ("Religious piety and beliefs are not only the source of Western morality but also the force that supports Western behavioral norms"), and the differential mode of association to Confucian ethics.[41]

Second, each link in a Chinese person's network is defined in terms of a dyadic social tie *(gang)*.[42] These interpersonal ties are

40. More recently, several scholars have considerably clarified the contrast between Western and Chinese religions and their effects on worldviews and social institutions. See Robert Bellah, "Father and Son in Christianity and Confucianism," in *Beyond Belief* (New York: Harper and Row, 1970), pp. 76–99; Joseph Needham, *Science and Civilisation in China* (Cambridge, England: Cambridge University Press, 1956), 2: 279–91; Marcel Granet, *The Religion of the Chinese People* (New York: Harper Torchbooks, 1977); Gary G. Hamilton, "Patriarchalism in Imperial China and Western Europe: A Revision of Weber's Sociology of Domination," *Theory and Society* 13, no. 3 (May 1984): 393–426, and "Patriarchy, Patrimonialism, and Filial Piety: A Comparison of China and Western Europe," *British Journal of Sociology* 41, no. 1 (March 1990): 77–104.

41. Chapter 5, p. 72. Confucianism's position in Chinese society is equivalent to Christianity's position in Western society. For a clear discussion of Confucianism, see Herbert Fingarette, *Confucius—The Secular as Sacred* (New York: Harper Torchbooks, 1972). For a recent debate on the origins of Western ideas that update Fei's very partial view of the West, see Louis Dumont, "A Modified View of Our Origins," *Religion* 12 (1982): 1–27, and the ensuing debate by Robert Bellah, S. N. Eisenstadt, and others.

42. What we have termed in English, synonymously, a "link," "tie," and "relationship" in Chinese can be translated in three ways: *lun, guanxi,* and *gang. Lun* and *guanxi* are normally translated as "relationship." "Relationship" in English, however, does not quite capture the binding quality suggested by the Chinese terms. The term "tie" captures the nature of social link better than "relationship" does. *Gang* is the term used to define the three closest relationships *(sangang)*: the ties between father and son, emperor and official, and husband and wife. *Gang,* which is the term for the lead rope of a fishing net, here means "guiding connections," suggesting that, as the basis of social order, the father guides the son, the emperor the official, and the husband the wife. For a discussion of the nature and historical development of these ties, see Hsu Dau-lin, "The Myth of the 'Five Human Relations' of Confucius," *Monumenta Serica* 29 (1970–71): 27–37. Also see Kwang-kuo Hwang, "Face and Favor: The Chinese Power Game," *American Journal of Sociology*

known in Chinese as *guanxi*.[43] Each tie is, simultaneously, both normatively defined and strictly personal. Each tie is normative in the sense that it consists of an explicit category of social relationship that requires specific, prescribed "ritual" (*li*) behavior. The tie is strictly personal in the sense that the specific prescribed actions needed to maintain the link are based on norms of reciprocity and are defined as personal obligations on the part of each individual, particularly the subordinate in the dyadic relationship: obligations of the child to the parent, the wife to the husband, the official to the ruler, and the younger to the older.

Third, networks have no explicit boundaries. Individuals do not sign up for "membership" in networks, as they might for a Western-style organization. They cannot enter and exit close social ties. Those ties are preset. Whether a person lives up to the obligations of those ties, and hence is "moral and upright," is another matter. Therefore, although the relationship preexists, a person is called upon to "achieve" the relationship by rising to the level of morality required by the specific tie.[44] Insofar as people uphold

---

92, no. 4 (January 1987): 944–74, for a description of the calculus of social ties in the Chinese context.

After this book had been completed, we learned of Ambrose Yeo-chi King's excellent essay on "Kuan-hsi and Network Building: A Sociological Interpretation," *Daedalus* 120, no. 2 (Spring 1991): 63–84. Drawing upon Fei and others, King describes *guanxi* and network building in ways similar to that found in this introduction.

43. *Guanxi* is conventionally translated into English as "relationship," but the term has many subtle meanings in a society whose social structure is created through strong and weak social relationships. In some locations, such as the People's Republic of China, *guanxi* has recently taken on the pejorative meaning of illegal backdoor connections with government officials. For an excellent analysis of the reemergence of traditional social networks and of *guanxi* ties in post-Mao China, see Thomas Gold, "After Comradeship," *China Quarterly*, no. 104 (1985): 657–75.

44. In one of the few efforts to evaluate and refine the concept of *chaxugeju*, Kao Cheng-shu, Peng Hwai-jen, and others in the Graduate Institute of Sociology at Tunghai University in Taiwan have argued that in Chinese society, a close relationship, even as close as that between a father and a son, should not be regarded as an *ascribed* characteristic. Instead, in their extensive studies of large family businesses, they have found that the differential mode of association in Chinese society is an important element of economic action in modern Taiwan, but a type of action that requires predictable, reciprocal behavior from all participants, with particular emphasis on the subordinate. All relationships are in some sense *achieved*. Even a son must prove, and must continue to prove, his reliability as a son to his father in order for the relationship to be fulfilled. See, in particular, Kao Cheng-shu, "The Role of 'Personal Trust' in Large Businesses in Taiwan," in *Business Networks and Economic Development in East and Southeast Asia*, ed. Gary G. Hamilton (Hong Kong: Centre of Asian Studies, 1991), and Peng Hwai-jen, *Taiwan qiye yezhu de 'guanxi' jiqi*

their obligations, a network built of strong and weak links can join people separated by considerable social and geographical distance. In principle, any two people can arrange a linkage through an intermediary or through a relational category in which they can situate themselves.[45] A society resting on networks contains no sharp boundary lines, but only ambiguous zones of more or less dense and more or less institutionalized network configurations.[46] Kinship networks are an example of a dense, well-institutionalized network configuration in Chinese society.

---

zhuanbian, yige shehuixue de fenxi (Relationships among Taiwan business owners and their changes: A sociological analysis) (unpublished dissertation, Tunghai University, 1989).

45. At times, one must use ingenuity to find the social grounds for a common relationship. For example, researchers in Taiwan have documented a proliferation of types of *guanxi*. They refer to this proliferation as *tongzhuyi* (sameism), in which any commonality can be used as a basis for a *guanxi* relationship that furthers the interests of the two parties. See Peng Hwai-jen, *Taiwan qiye yezhu de 'guanxi' jiqi zhuanbian*. Mayfair Mei-hui Yang makes much the same point for the People's Republic of China: "In the art of *guanxi*, this transformation [from the unfamiliar to the familiar] occurs in the process of appealing to shared identities between persons—hence the emphasis on 'shared' (*tong*) qualities and experiences that shape the identities of classmates (*tongxue*), fellow townsmen (or persons from the same county or province) (*tongxiang*), colleagues (*tongshi*), as well as kinfolk and those in the teacher-student and master-apprentice relationships, etcetera. Familiarity, then, is born of the fusion of personal identities. And shared identities establish the basis for the obligation and compulsion to share one's wealth and to help with one's labor" ("The Gift Economy and State Power in China," *Comparative Studies in Society and History* 31, no. 1 [January 1989]: 40–41).

46. Kao Cheng-shu's analysis of modern Taiwan is very suggestive on this point: "Most social connections among businessmen are with relatives, friends, colleagues, and former classmates. All these relationships are traditional and personal, and rarely have anything to do with 'class.' Such traditional lines of relationship serve to weaken the formation and development of class consciousness. . . . A middle class businessman usually relies on factional consideration when choosing a business partner or a political candidate. 'Class' benefits will not figure into these decisions. Chinese think in terms of more personalized relationships, which play major roles in daily life, not in vague notions of class. . . . At present, because traditional relationship networks still dominate daily personal and social life, generalized concepts such as 'middle class' are less helpful in explaining the island's economic, political, and social structures" ("Power Diminished by Ambiguity," *Free China Review* 39, no. 11 [November 1989]: 7).

This article is extracted from a longer article. For the original, see "Dui fujian Taiwan 'zhongchan jieji' de jidian guancha" (Some considerations in the investigation of Taiwan's middle class), in *Bianqian zhong Taiwan shehui de zhongchan jieji* (The middle class in changing Taiwan society), ed. Xiao Xin-huang (Taipei: Chuliu Books, 1989), pp. 21–31. Also see two other particularly fine treatments of network structures in Taiwan: Susan Greenhalgh, "Networks and Their Nodes: Urban Society in Taiwan," *China Quarterly* 99 (September 1984): 529–52; and J. Bruce Jacobs, "A Preliminary Model of Particularistic Ties in Chinese Political Alliances," *China Quarterly* 78 (1979): 237–73.

Fourth, the moral content of behavior in a network society is situation specific.[47] Embedded in a world of differentially categorized social relationships, people evaluate ongoing action by considering the specific relations among actors. What is considered moral behavior depends on the situation and on the social categories of the actors, rather than on abstract standards pertaining to autonomous individuals. Shun, the legendary emperor of China, would be morally obligated to run away with his father, a murderer, to prevent his father's arrest.[48]

In sum, *chaxugeju* (the differential mode of association) is the term that Fei uses to depict an egocentric system of social networks linking people together in multiple ways and placing different, though clear-cut, moral demands on each person in each specific context. Fei points out clearly that Chinese society is not group oriented—a view that is contrary to most modern interpretations. Instead, Chinese society is centered on the individual and is built from networks created from relational ties linking the self with discrete categories of other individuals.[49] This is a society in which considerations of order, not laws, predominate; and in this context, order means—to paraphrase the *Xiaojing* (The classic on filial piety)—that each person must uphold the moral obligations of his or her network ties. Otherwise, the entire social system collapses.[50]

SELF AND SOCIETY

Using the contrasting theoretical models of Chinese and Western societies developed in chapter 4, Fei widens the scope of his analy-

47. For a good description of the situational logic of interpersonal behavior, see Kwang-kuo Hwang, "Face and Favor: The Chinese Power Game," *American Journal of Sociology* 92, no. 4 (January 1987): 944–74; and Yang, "Gift Economy and State Power in China." For an excellent case study of morality in action, and one that makes good use of Fei's theory of morality in *Xiangtu Zhongguo*, see Richard Madsen, *Morality and Power in a Chinese Village* (Berkeley: University of California Press, 1984).

48. See chapter 5, p. 77.

49. For one of the best recent discussions of this topic, one that draws its theoretical core from *Xiangtu Zhongguo*, see Ambrose Y. C. King, "The Individual and Group in Confucianism: A Relational Perspective," in *Individualism and Holism*, ed. Donald Munro (Ann Arbor: Center for Chinese Studies, University of Michigan, 1985), pp. 57–70. Also see Hajime Nakamura's discussion in *Ways of Thinking of Eastern Peoples* (Honolulu: University of Hawaii Press, 1971), pp. 247–58.

50. For a pertinent analysis of the logic of obedience in the Chinese context, including an analysis of the *Xiaojing*, see Hamilton, "Patriarchalism in Imperial China and Western Europe." The *Xiaojing* was written by an unknown author in the Han dynasty (206 B.C.–A.D. 220) and later became a widely read text on filial obedience.

sis to other aspects of society. Throughout the remainder of the book, he pays particular attention to the composition of the self, to social psychology, and to the logic of social action.

The self in Chinese society is embedded in social relationships and is emotionally tied to personal obligations as defined by those relationships.[51] To conceptualize a Chinese notion of self in society, Fei several times repeats the Confucian maxim *ke ji fu li* (subdue the self and follow the rites). By this maxim, Fei emphasizes that *human* nature and truly *human* conduct always entail living up to one's obligations as defined by one's social relationships. To be a human in Chinese society is to be linked to others—to one's parents, siblings, children, and friends—and to fulfill the obligations of those linkages. To do otherwise is to be less than human. Being embedded in social relationships, a self is discovered only through a person's role as son or daughter, husband or wife, father or mother, brother or sister, and friend. There is, in principle, no self outside of roles and relationships.[52] Accordingly, Chinese society is one in which individuality is restrained, and emotions, particularly the emotions toward people of the opposite sex, are controlled.

The self in Western society is no less socially constructed than it is in Asia, but it is, in principle, a soul-bearing self, a unique entity that is permanently and intrinsically linked to no human, only to

51. Recent studies of Chinese notions of self have supported Fei's conclusions. See, for instance, Mark Elvin, "Between the Earth and Heaven: Conceptions of Self in China," in *The Category of the Person*, ed. Michael Carrithers, Steven Collins, and Steven Lukes (Cambridge, England: Cambridge University Press, 1985); Robert E. Hegel and Richard C. Hessney (eds.), *Expressions of Self in Chinese Literature* (New York: Columbia University Press, 1985); Frederick W. Mote, "The Arts and the 'Theorizing Mode' of the Civilization," in *Artists and Traditions: Uses of the Past in Chinese Culture*, ed. Christian F. Murck (Princeton, N.J.: Princeton University Press, 1976); Tu Wei-ming, *Confucian Thought: Selfhood as Creative Transformation* (Albany, N.Y.: State University of New York Press, 1985); Arthur Wright, "Values, Roles, and Personalities," in *Confucian Personalities*, ed. Arthur Wright and Denis Twitchett (Stanford, Calif.: Stanford University Press, 1962); and Wu Pei-yi, "Varieties of the Chinese Self," in *Designs of Selfhood*, ed. Vytautas Kavolis (London: Associated University Press, 1984). Also see Hsien Chin Hu, "The Chinese Concept of 'Face,' " *American Anthropologist* 46 (1944): 45–64.

52. The use of the word *role* in this context needs to be qualified. In Western society, the term implies that a person "plays" a part but is also separate from the part. Psychologically and sociologically, there is presumed to be—in theory though not always in fact—a "distance" between the person and the role. In the Chinese context, the society, in theory, provides no distance between the person and the role; they are one and the same. Hence, the term *role* is somewhat misleading, but English provides few alternatives. For a theoretical discussion of some of these issues in regard to role theory, see Ralph Turner, "The Role and the Person," *American Journal of Sociology* 84, no. 1 (July 1978): 1–23.

God.[53] It is a self that defines its identity in society through willed emotional attachments and voluntary organizational member-ships. The presumed autonomy of the self and the necessity to anchor one's self in a social world make it incumbent on each in-dividual to discover or create his or her "true" self.[54] At a social psychological level, then, a person is required to activate the self through the exercise of will and to shape the self through personal experiences, through "an effort to create the meaning of life it-self."[55] Fei describes this process as a "Faustian" struggle of indi-viduals to realize themselves by being separate from, and rising above, all social roles. In this context, Fei shows that the Western idea of "love" plays an important part in the creation of the West-ern self but is less important in—and sometimes detrimental to—the creation and maintenance of families.[56]

As part of this discussion of Chinese and Western models of self in society, Fei outlines a comparative theory of gender and sex roles.[57] Modern Western ideas of individual autonomy lead people to conceive of themselves as distinct from all social roles and to regard biological roles as narrow and, except for sex and reproduc-tion, secondary. In Chinese society, however, gender definitions are an intrinsic aspect of the categorization of relationships. To il-lustrate the Chinese context, Fei cites the ancient prescription "Be-

53. See Bellah, "Father and Son," and Tu Wei-ming, *Confucian Thought*, for a more detailed comparison between Chinese and Western views of the self.
54. For an excellent discussion of this phenomenon in American society, see Ralph Turner, "The Real Self: From Institution to Impulse," *American Journal of Sociology* 81, no. 5 (March 1976): 989–1016.
55. Chapter 7, p. 91.
56. For some recent work on the notion of "love" (*ai*), which suggests that its modern meaning in Chinese society is very recent and is largely the result of the diffusion of Western culture, see, for instance, Jai Ben-ray, "Xifang sixiang zhong de 'ai' guan" (The image of 'love' in Western thought), *Zhongguo wenhua yuekan* 75 (January 1986): 94–110.
57. Recent research in this area substantiates Fei's early ideas. See, e.g., Mar-gery Wolf and Roxanne Witke, eds. *Women in Chinese Society* (Stanford, Calif.: Stan-ford University Press, 1975); Judith Stacey, *Patriarchy and Socialist Revolution in China* (Berkeley: University of California Press, 1983); Tani Barlow, "Gender and Identity in Ding Ling's Mother," *Modern Chinese Literature* 3, no. 1 (Spring 1987): 7–17, and "Woman in Ding Ling's World: Writing, Feminism, and Difference in Revolution-ary China" (unpublished manuscript, 1989); Ann Anagnost, "Transformations of Gender in Modern China," in *Gender and Anthropology: Critical Reviews for Research and Teaching*, ed. Sandra Morgen (Washington, D.C.: American Anthropological Association, 1989), pp. 313–29. Also see Emily Honig and Gail Hershatter, *Personal Voices* (Stanford, Calif.: Stanford University Press, 1988), a compilation of women speaking about their own lives in the People's Republic of China in the 1980s.

tween men and women, there are only differences." In Chinese society, gender definitions cannot be separated from social roles; gender definitions are inherent aspects of relational categories and are primal forces fundamental in shaping the world—the *yin* and the *yang*.[58] In Chinese society, it is difficult to conceive of "man" and "woman" as meaningful social categories apart from specific relationships.[59] In the West, however, "man" and "woman" are *the* meaningful categories, but the social roles that go with them are always open for reexamination and redefinition.

POWER AND THE NETWORK STRUCTURE OF SOCIETY

In addition to his emphasis on the social psychological level of social action, Fei emphasizes some of the structural dimensions of social action. In this context, he primarily analyzes the exercise of power in the structures that make up society.

Implicitly, Fei continues to use his contrasting "modes of association" to discuss Chinese social structure. Power, in the sense of how people control and are controlled by others, is configured in a very different way in Chinese society than it is in Western society.[60] In the West, where individuals are presumed to be autonomous and hence necessarily able to exercise their will, authority (the right to exercise power) is based on a rule of law. Individual rights, as identified in and secured through a constitution, specify

58. See Richard J. Smith, *China's Cultural Heritage: The Ch'ing Dynasty, 1644–1912* (Boulder, Colo.: Westview Press, 1983), pp. 100–108, which has a particularly good discussion of the *yin-yang* classification. As he stresses, "The important point to keep in mind is that *yin* and *yang* were always viewed as relative concepts. As creative forces they were continually in flux, each growing out of the other and each in turn 'controlling' situations or activities. . . . In the main, then, *yin* and *yang* were not things, but classifications of relations. Any given object or phenomenon might be designated *yin* in one set of relations and *yang* in another" (p. 103).

59. Tani Barlow, "Woman in Ding Ling's World," pp. 7–39, and Ann Anagnost, "Transformations of Gender in Modern China," make this point as well.

60. Recent research on power is largely independent of Fei's influence but confirms his early conclusions. See, in particular, S. R. Schram, *The Scope of State Power in China* (Hong Kong: Chinese University Press, 1985). Also see Lucian W. Pye, *Asian Power and Politics: The Cultural Dimensions of Authority* (Cambridge, Mass.: Harvard University Press, 1985); Romeyn Taylor, "Chinese Hierarchy in Comparative Perspective," *Journal of Asian Studies* 48, no. 3 (August 1989): 490–511; and Hamilton, "Patriarchalism in Imperial China and Western Europe," and "Heaven Is High and the Emperor Is Far Away: Legitimacy and Structure in the Chinese State," *Revue européenne des sciences sociales* 27, no. 84 (1989): 141–67.

the basis of individual autonomy. Laws itemize those actions that would unduly infringe on the autonomy of individuals. Hence, laws define what should not be done. Breaking the law consists of some action that expressly violates individual rights.

In contrast, Chinese society is ruled through rituals.[61] Order in this kind of society depends primarily on people's obedience to their principal social obligations. Therefore, the social obligations for every category of relationship must be spelled out, the people must be taught about those obligations, and "correction" must be meted out for any failure to learn.[62] The unit of control is the dyadic relationship, and not the individual, as is the case with a rule of law. Therefore, the entire network of people joined through a set of relationships is implicated in any one person's failure to perform appropriately.[63] As Fei points out, control in this system is a shared responsibility, in that everyone supervises the actions of others, and also is internalized in each person, in that each person conceives of obedience to relationships as self-control—as an aspect of an individual's responsibility to, and self-realization in, his own social roles.

The logic and the actual unit of control (the person versus the

61. Recent research confirms this conclusion. The clearest statement has been made by Leon Vandermeersch, "An Enquiry into the Chinese Conception of the Law," in Schram, *The Scope of State Power*, pp. 3–25. Also see Kwang-Ching Liu, ed. *Orthodoxy in Late Imperial China* (Berkeley: University of California Press, 1990). For a particularly clear demonstration of the network structure of Chinese political alliances, see Jacobs, "A Preliminary Model of Particularistic Ties in Chinese Political Alliances."

62. This idea is discussed broadly in Hamilton, "Patriarchalism in Imperial China and Western Europe" and "Patriarchy, Patrimonialism, and Filial Piety."

63. This point could not be better illustrated than by an example that Hsu Dau-lin gives in "The Myth of the 'Five Human Relations' of Confucius," pp. 36–37: "In October 1865, Cheng Han-cheng's wife had the insolence to beat her mother-in-law. This was regarded as such a heinous crime that the following punishment was meted out. Cheng and his wife were both skinned alive, in front of the mother, their skin was displayed at the city gates in various towns and their bones burned to ashes. Cheng's grand uncle, the eldest of his close relatives, was beheaded; his uncle and two brothers, and the head of the Cheng clan, were hanged. The wife's mother, her face tatooed with the words 'neglecting her daughter's education,' was paraded through seven provinces. Her father was beaten 80 strokes and banished to a distance of 3000 *li*. The heads of family in the houses to the right and the left of the Chengs' were beaten 80 strokes and banished to Heilongjiang. The educational officer in town was beaten 60 strokes and banished to a distance of 1000 *li*. Cheng's nine-month-old boy was given a new name and put in the county magistrate's care. Cheng's land was to be left in waste 'forever.' All this was recorded on a stone stele and rubbings of the inscriptions were distributed throughout the empire."

relationship) differ in Chinese and Western societies.[64] Given this difference, it is not surprising to find that the political institutions in these two locations also differ.[65] According to Fei, the state, as the constitutional embodiment of its people, is the highest level of organization in Western society. It is a compulsory organization, in which people are forced to claim membership. The state establishes laws and guarantees them; the state is the essence of legitimacy, and all power holders, even parents within families, obtain their *rights* to control others within specified jurisdictional boundaries from the state and from the legal framework that the state upholds.[66]

In China, however, the state does not exist as an organization. The fundamental nexus of control is not a jurisdictional top-down system that controls the actions of every individual through the imposition of rules. Instead, the means of control is located in the institutionalized networks of relationships—in the patriarchal control of the family, in the elders' control of villages, and in the notables' control of other kinds of associational networks.[67] As Fei explains, power holders' authority derives from their "educational" function. They maintain order by upholding the morality of differential relationships in which they themselves hold a superordinate position. Because they hold a superordinate role and likely

64. See note 51 above.

65. For the most recent, as well as the best, work on this topic, see Schram, *The Scope of State Power;* also see Taylor, "Chinese Hierarchy in Comparative Perspective," and Hamilton, "Heaven Is High and the Emperor Is Far Away."

66. See Jennifer Nedolsky, "Law, Boundaries, and the Bounded Self," *Representations* 30 (Spring 1990): 162–89, for a fine discussion of the conceptions of self in a legal rational society.

67. Prasenjit Duara, in *Culture, Power, and the State: Rural North China, 1900–1942* (Stanford, Calif.: Stanford University Press, 1988), has recently "rediscovered" many of these points and has persuasively argued for a reconceptualization of power in China: "The point is that these principles [of power] cannot exhaustively be understood by a single overarching system, such as the marketing system or any other *system.* Rather, together they form an intersecting, seamless nexus stretching across the many particular boundaries of settlements and organizations. . . . Organizations in North China . . . were interlocked in various ways, including personal relationships in informal networks that acted as the weft linking key points in these organizations. Power in local society tended to be concentrated at the densest points of interaction—the nodes of greatest coordination within the nexus," (p. 16). For other discussions of systems of control in China, see Frederic Wakeman, Jr., and Carolyn Grant (eds.), *Conflict and Control in Late Imperial China* (Berkeley: University of California Press, 1975), and Sybille van der Sprenkel, "Urban Social Control," in *The City in Late Imperial China*, ed. G. William Skinner (Stanford, Calif.: Stanford University Press, 1977), pp. 609–32.

do so in multiple networks of relationships (e.g., family and village), certain power holders become responsible for everyone's proper conduct in the network. The more distant one is from the core of a network, the less one can legitimately arbitrate the conduct of people in the network.

Fei describes state institutions in Chinese society with the saying "Heaven is high and the emperor is far away." Although political officials may have educational, coordinating, and even corrective roles, they are distant from local society and have circumscribed duties in relation to it. In principle, officials are responsible for managing the whole, but they do not intervene in the parts.[68] The only exception occurs when the parts threaten the stability of the whole. When disorder occurs, all within that immediate network are at fault, and each successive circle has a duty to intervene and reestablish order. When families fight, village and lineage councils must intervene and punish everyone concerned, as Fei illustrates. But were disorder to encompass the village, then the county or the provincial authorities could legitimately intervene and could even destroy the village. Parents, therefore, must correct the mistakes of their children; lineages, of their kinsmen; village elders, of their fellow villagers; merchants, of their fellow merchants; and officials, of their fellow officials. Even the rulers' chief duty has been to put their own households in order. The logic, of course, is that if everyone supervises and upholds the morality of his or her close relations, then the entire world is at rest and people can prosper. The ideal government should *wuwei*—do nothing.

As Fei describes them, Chinese political institutions work in the way his metaphor about the spreading ripples of water would suggest: from the inside out. Institutions of control in families and lineages are more important for establishing social order than are those in locales, which are in turn more important than those in more distant government locations. Chinese social structure works in the same way. Ties of kinship and locale create core sets of egocentric networks, which individuals can manipulate and expand to take advantage of economic and other kinds of opportunities. The key example Fei discusses is the family enterprise. Western fami-

---

68. For an excellent collection of studies that explore the state's use of culture as a strategy of rulership, see Kwang-Ching Liu, *Orthodoxy in Late Imperial China*.

lies are organizations with fixed members, but Chinese families are networks capable of expanding outward. These networks are without clear boundaries and consist of differential categories of kinship relations.[69] The closest relationships, such as those between parents and children, are normally the most reliable and predictable, because they are also the most controlled, both internally and externally. These ties provide critical resources for economic enterprises.[70]

From this relational core, Chinese families extend themselves into the economy.[71] They make no distinction between family and firm, and normally they do business at a distance, both physical and social, from others with whom they have close obligations. Normally, they migrate to enter commercial professions, and in that new setting they create regional ties with others from the same broadly defined native place.[72] As Fei says, the use of native-place relationships is "the projection of consanguinity into space"[73]— that is, the ability to link with others who are not close relatives

69. For good summaries of the literature on Chinese kinship, see James L. Watson, "Chinese Kinship Reconsidered: Anthropological Perspectives on Historical Research," *China Quarterly* 92 (December 1982): 589–627; Hugh Baker, *Chinese Family and Kinship* (New York: Columbia University Press, 1979); Hsieh Jih-chang and Chuang Ying-chang, *The Chinese Family and Its Ritual Behavior* (Taipei: Institute of Ethnology, Academia Sinica, 1985).

70. That the Chinese use their families for enterprise has been substantiated in recent research. For some of the best recent examples, see Lau Siu-kai's discussion of the Chinese "utilitarian" family in *Society and Politics in Hong Kong* (Hong Kong: Chinese University Press, 1982) and Wong Siu-lun's discussion of the entrepreneurial family in "The Applicability of Asian Family Values to Other Socio-cultural Settings," in *In Search of an East Asian Development Model*, ed. Peter Berger and Michael Hsiao (New Brunswick, N.J.: Transaction Books, 1988), pp. 134–52.

71. For some recent research on the family as the core of Chinese enterprise, all of which supports Fei's thesis, see Wong Siu-lun, "The Chinese Family Firm: A Model," *British Journal of Sociology* 36, no. 1 (March 1985): 58–72; Gordon Redding, *The Spirit of Chinese Capitalism* (Berlin: de Gruyter, 1990); John Omohundro, *Chinese Merchant Families in Iloilo* (Athens: Ohio University Press, 1981); Gary G. Hamilton and Kao Cheng-shu, "The Institutional Foundations of Chinese Business: The Family Firm in Taiwan," *Comparative Social Research* 12 (1990): 95–112; Victor Nee, "Peasant Household Individualism," in *Chinese Rural Development: The Great Transformation*, ed. William L. Parish (Armonk, N.Y.: M. E. Sharpe, 1985); Victor Nee and Su Sijin, "Institutional Change and Economic Growth in China," *Journal of Asian Studies* 49 (1990): 3–25.

72. Recent research on this topic confirms Fei's insights. See, for example, G. William Skinner, "Mobility Strategies in Late Imperial China: A Regional Systems Analysis," in *Regional Analysis*, ed. Carol A. Smith (New York: Academic Press, 1976); Gary G. Hamilton, "Why No Capitalism in China," in *Max Weber in Asian Studies*, ed. Andreas E. Buss (Leiden: E. J. Brill, 1985).

73. Chapter 12, p. 123.

but who, for the purposes of business, can be trusted as if they were relatives. In the past two centuries, the Chinese have become merchants to the world, largely because they have been able to create highly efficient, flexible commercial networks.[74] These networks consist of tightly connected family firms linked into geographically dispersed, loosely connected native-place networks.

Chinese social structure is unlike Western social structure. Fei's metaphors suggest the difference. In the West, social structures consist of a framework of organizations, which individuals can join and leave when they want to. These organizations vary in degree of formality (from those with explicit written rules to those with only tacit understandings about conduct) and openness (from totally open to entirely closed groups). Moreover, organizations also vary according to the social composition of their members (rich or poor, high or low status), and thus organizations typically reflect a society's class structure. By contrast, Chinese society consists not of organizations arranged systematically in society but, rather, as Fei put it, of "webs woven out of countless personal relationships."[75] These multiple sets of expandable, ego-centered networks link everyone in society in a variety of ways with varying strengths of attachment. In general, the higher a person's prestige (and perhaps wealth), the more likely that person will have a dense web of horizontal and vertical network ties. Moreover, the more linkages one maintains, the more intensively one is wedged into an existing social order and is committed to the status quo.

Social change is very difficult in this context. Chinese cannot simply change networks in the same way that Westerners join or leave organizations. Networks ride on set categories of relationship. The key factor in the network structure of Chinese society is that one's obligations to family and kinship networks override the obligations to more distant network ties.[76] Therefore, as Fei argues, the Chinese lineage networks, which center on the household, are

74. This phenomenon is well illustrated in various studies of the rapid industrialization in Chinese society outside the People's Republic of China. See, for instance, Linda Y. C. Lim and L. A. Peter Gosling (eds.), *The Chinese in Southeast Asia* (Singapore: Maruzen Asia, 1983), and Hamilton, *Business Networks and Economic Development in East and Southeast Asia.*

75. Chapter 5, p. 78.

76. See, for instance, Kwang-kuo Hwang, "Face and Favor: The Chinese Power Game."

the "medium through which all activities are organized."[77] These family and kinship connections form "inner" networks. These, in turn, overlap in numerous ways with sets of "outer" networks consisting of fellow regionals, classmates, friends of friends. Desire, opportunity, and success are bound up with obedience to these inner and outer network obligations. Subordinates cannot easily initiate change, and superordinates cannot readily abandon relationships and still perpetuate their importance and centrality. In short, people do not lead networks in the same way that people lead organizations.

CONCLUSION

Fei's theory of Chinese society describes a society founded on social relationships and interlocking social networks. From reading *Xiangtu Zhongguo*, one does not know whether these patterns are unique to Chinese society or whether other non-Western societies might contain similar network structures.[78] Even Fei intimates, at times, that the basic contrast is between traditional rural societies and modern urban societies. But at other times, such as when he develops the Confucian logic of social relationships and situational morality, Fei seems to argue that Chinese society has truly distinctive organizational principles. As he fully acknowledges, however, his theory is a first step; working through the comparative implications of Fei's work is an important task for future research. However, it is equally clear that, if Fei's description of China is correct (and there seems to be plenty of subsequent research supporting Fei's views), the analysis of Chinese society also needs to be reassessed: China should be considered not a class-based but a network-based society; thus, the conventional and ubiquitous class

77. Chapter 6, p. 84.
78. There is sufficient evidence to indicate that the network patterns described by Fei are distinctively Chinese. Even in Japan, which is geographically in the same region and historically linked in numerous ways, social organization rests on very different relational principles. In her book *Japanese Society* (Berkeley: University of California Press, 1970, p. 13), Chie Nakane discusses some of the differences between Japanese and Chinese social organization. In his very fine discussion of "Kuanhsi and Network Building," Ambrose Yeo-chi King explains this contrast between the two societies in more detail.

analyses of Chinese society may need to be revised.[79] This, too, may be an important task for future research.

The notion that China is not a class-based society went directly against the Marxist interpretation that Mao and others were applying to China at the same time that Fei wrote *Xiangtu Zhongguo*. This apparent contradiction caused Fei much personal trouble from the 1950s until the end of the Cultural Revolution, and even afterward. Mao's star, however, has now set. Mao's statues, once a prominent feature in Chinese city squares, have been toppled in many places, and his once ubiquitous portraits have disappeared. Marxist analysis, however, is still orthodoxy. Accordingly, Fei's early writings have had only limited influence in the PRC, and only a few have been reissued.

Outside the PRC, especially in Hong Kong and Taiwan, Fei's sociology is coming into its own. His concepts, many of them from *Xiangtu Zhongguo*, have greatly contributed to Chinese social scientists' views of Chinese society today. To the Chinese themselves, it is a transformative view; Fei's theories have become the points of reference for how to think about Chinese society.

For Westerners who read this book and who think through Fei's ideas for the first time, Fei's view is equally transformative. Here is a clear demonstration that what passes in the West for general social theory is often, in fact, local knowledge—particular rules about particular people in particular places. Fei's sociology demands that we in the West rethink ourselves.

79. In fairness, it should be noted that Mao used class analysis as a way to change Chinese society, to mobilize the peasantry, rather than as a way to understand it. Mao's idea was to use Marxism to break through the old relational bonds of society, which he labeled "feudalistic," and to create new categories for rebuilding the social order. Also see note 45.

FROM THE SOIL

1

Special Characteristics of Rural Society

Chinese society is fundamentally rural. I say that it is fundamentally rural because its foundation is rural. Several variations have arisen from this foundation, but even so, these variations retain their rural character. Moreover, in the past hundred years, a very special society has formed as a consequence of the encounter between East and West.[1] For the time being, however, I am not going to discuss the characteristics of these variations, but instead will concentrate exclusively on rural society and on those so-called hayseeds, the people living in the countryside. They are truly the foundation of Chinese society.

We often say that country people are figuratively as well as literally "soiled" (tuqi). Although this label may seem disrespectful, the character meaning "soil" (tu) is appropriately used here. Country people cannot do without the soil because their very livelihood is based upon it. In the earliest times, there may have been some groups of people in the Far East who did not know how to farm; but for us now, how those primitives lived is merely a matter of curiosity. Today, most people in East Asia make a living by working in the fields. To be more specific, even from early times, the tributaries of China's three large rivers were already entirely agricultural.[2] Historically, wherever people from those agricultural regions migrated, they took with them their tradition of making a living from the soil.

Note: Unless otherwise indicated, all footnotes to the text are provided by the translators.

1. Fei is alluding to three interrelated variations of Chinese society in the twentieth century. In addition to rural society, which he sees as the foundation for the other two variations, he distinguishes urban society and coastal Westernized society. For his discussion of these variations, see Xiangtu chongjian (Reconstructing rural China) (Xianggang: Wenxue chubanshe, n.d.), pp. 16–23.

2. The three rivers to which Fei refers are the Yangtze, the Yellow, and the Wei.

Recently, I met an American friend who had returned from a trip to Inner Mongolia. He told me he could not understand why the people who moved to those frontier prairies still tried to farm as if they lived in China's heartland. Mongolian grasslands are best suited only for pastureland, but he said that every family had carved up the land into small plots for farming. It was as if they had dived, headfirst, into the soil, as if they were unable to see any other way of using the land. I remember that one of my teachers, Dr. Shiro-kogoroff, once told me about some Chinese who had moved to Siberia. In total disregard of the climate, those Chinese still planted their seeds just to see if anything would grow. These accounts show that the Chinese are really inseparable from the soil. To be sure, out of this soil has grown a glorious history, but it is a history that was naturally limited by what could be taken from the soil. Now it appears that these very limitations imposed by agriculture will hold China back, will prevent the nation from moving forward.

Only those who make a living from the soil can understand the value of soil. City dwellers scorn country people for their closeness to the land; they treat them as if they were truly "soiled." But to country people, the soil is the root of their lives. In rural areas, the god represented in the most shrines is Tudi, the god of the earth. Tudi is the god closest to human nature; Tudi and his wife are an old white-haired couple who take care of all the business of the countryside and who have come to symbolize the earth itself. When I went abroad for the first time, my nanny slipped something wrapped in red paper into the bottom of my suitcase. Later, she told me in private that if I had trouble getting accustomed to my new home and if I were too homesick, I should make some soup from the stuff wrapped in the red paper. In the package was dirt that she had scraped from her stove. I remember seeing a similar custom in a movie called *A Song to Remember*, which took place in Poland, an Eastern European agricultural country. It made me re-alize even more what an important role the earth plays and should play in a civilization like ours.

Agriculture differs from both pastoralism and industry. Farmers are necessarily connected to the land, whereas herdsmen drift about, following the water and the grass, and are forever unsettled. In-dustrial workers may choose where they live, and they may move without difficulty; but farmers cannot move their land or the crops they grow. Always waiting for their crops to mature, those old farmers seem to have planted half their own bodies into the soil; it is this inability to move that causes farmers to appear so backward and sedentary.

Indeed, those who must depend on farming seem to be stuck in the soil. I once met a friend who had studied language in the Zhang Bei area of northern China.[3] I asked him if the language there had been influenced by Mongolian. Shaking his head, he said that no influence at all could be seen, in language or in any other aspect. "For hundreds of years," he noted, "there have always been only a few surnames in the village. I reconstructed the genealogy of each family from the gravestones, and it is clear that only these few families have ever lived there. The entire population of the village seems rooted in the soil; generation after generation, not much appears to have changed." We could add some qualifications to his conclusion, but, generally speaking, this kind of attachment to the soil is one of the characteristics of rural society. It is normal for farmers to settle in one spot for generations; it would be abnormal for them to migrate. Of course, droughts, floods, or continuous wars may force some farmers to leave their homes. But even such big events as the war of resistance against Japan did not, I believe, produce high mobility among rural people.

I certainly do not mean to argue that the rural population of China is fixed. That is impossible, because the population increases so quickly. After only several generations of normal reproduction, the number of people on one piece of land reaches a saturation point. The surplus population has to leave; those people, all carrying their own hoes, go out to open up new lands. But the core groups seldom move. And those who do migrate, if they find the land to survive, like the seeds blown from the trees by the wind, create the same small, lineage-based villages that they left behind. Those who do not find land simply vanish, or perhaps go into business. While I was in Guangxi province, near the mountains where the Yao people live, I saw some migrant villages—seeds that had been blown from the old trees—where people had to struggle bitterly to create a home from new soil. In Yunnan province, I saw other small villages that had been in existence for only two or three

3. Zhang Bei is a county in northwestern Hebei province.

generations. In the same places, I have also seen homeless vagrants who failed to find any land at all, and some dead bodies, half eaten by dogs, along the sides of the road.

This immobility, this enduring attachment to the soil, points to a relationship between people and space. Being fixed in space, people live in solitude and isolation. But the unit of isolation is not the individual but the group. For farming, it is not necessary for many people to live together. The division of labor required for agriculture is very simple. At most, there are a few distinctions between what men and women do; women typically transplant rice seedlings, whereas men usually hoe the soil. But this kind of cooperation is not designed to achieve greater efficiency; rather, it occurs because during the busy farming season there are just too many things for men to do by themselves, so their families come out to the fields to help them. Because farming has not developed a specialized division of labor, it is unnecessary for many people to live together in the same place. Therefore, when we see various sizes of rural communities, we may be sure that many of the larger ones were formed for reasons other than agriculture.

The smallest rural communities can be as small as one household. A husband, a wife, and some children, living together, fulfill the need for sex and procreation. In any kind of society, except for such special cases as armies and schools, the family is always the most basic social unit. In China's countryside, however, communities with only one family are seldom seen. There may be some such communities in terraced mountainous areas of Sichuan, but the majority of farmers live grouped together in villages. This pattern of residence greatly influences the nature of Chinese rural society. In rural areas of the United States, each family is geographically separated from its neighbors and constitutes its own individual collectivity. This pattern is the consequence of the early frontier period, when the land was vast and the people few. In those days, settlers held fast to a spirit of individual responsibility and self-reliance. In China, the same situation would be very rare. Generally speaking, Chinese farmers live grouped together in villages for the following reasons: (1) The piece of land that each family cultivates is invariably small. This is a petty agricultural economy; people live together in the same place so that they can be close to their fields. (2) Where irrigation is required, people must work together as a group, so living together is quite convenient. (3) Living together as a group also greatly contributes to everyone's security. (4) We practice partible inheritance of land, which gives an equal share of an estate to all male heirs. Therefore, because of this practice of dividing land among brothers, and thus attaching each of them to the same soil, over a period of several generations small communities grow into large villages.

[No matter what the reasons, the basic unit of Chinese rural society is the village.] Some villages may have only three households; others may have as many as several thousand households. When I mentioned that a characteristic of Chinese rural society is solitude and isolation, I was referring to the situation of villages, not individuals. The solitude and isolation are, of course, not absolute. But because villagers do not move around much, the communities themselves do not interact much. I think it is safe to say that life in rural society is very parochial. Villagers restrict the scope of their daily activities; they do not travel far; they seldom make contact with the outside world; they live solitary lives; they maintain their own isolated social circle. All of these characteristics contribute to the parochialism of rural China.

People in rural China know no other life than that dictated by their own parochialism. It is a society where people live from birth to death in the same place, and where people think that this is the normal way of life. Because everyone in a village lives like that, distinctive patterns of human relationships form. Every child grows up in everyone else's eyes, and in the child's eyes everyone and everything seem ordinary and habitual. This is a society without strangers, a society based totally on the familiar.

In sociology, we usually make a distinction between two basic types of societies. [One type of society forms as a natural result of people growing up together, and has no other purpose than being simply an outgrowth of human interaction. The other type of society is that which has been organized explicitly to fulfill goals. In the words of the German sociologist Ferdinand Toennies, the first type is called *Gemeinschaft* and the second *Gesellschaft*.[4] To the French sociologist Emile Durkheim, the first is an example of mechanical

4. Ferdinand Toennies, *Community and Association*, trans. Charles P. Loomis (London: Routledge and Kegan Paul, 1955).

solidarity and the second an example of organic solidarity.[5] Using our own terms, we would identify the first type of society as one based on ritual and customs *(lisu)* and the second as one based on law and reason *(fali)*. Later on, I will carefully analyze the differences between these two societies, but for now I merely want to emphasize that the land itself constrains the lives of rural people. The people they see every day are the ones they have known since childhood, just as they know the people in their own families. They do not have to select the kind of society they would live in; they are born into it; choice is not a factor.

Familiarity is an intimate feeling that develops from frequent and repeated interaction occurring over a long period of time. The character used in the first sentence of Confucius's *Analects* expresses this process of interaction. The character is *xi*, which means "to practice." If we put this character together with *xue*, which means "to meet strange things for the first time," we obtain the idea "to learn" *(xuexi)*. First we encounter, then we practice; and through this process, the unknown becomes the familiar. One obtains a real sense of satisfaction from becoming thoroughly intimate with one's environment. In a society characterized by this level of familiarity, we achieve a level of freedom whereby we can do whatever we please without fear of violating the norms of the society. This type of freedom is unlike those freedoms defined and protected by laws. The social norms in a familiar society rest not upon laws but, rather, upon rituals and customs that are defined through practice; hence, to follow these norms is to follow one's own heart and mind *(xin)*. In other words, society and the individual become one.

"We all know each other very well *(shuren)*. If you need my help, you have it. You don't have to ask twice." Expressions such as these expose the limitations of our modern society. Modern society is composed of strangers. We do not know each other's pasts. When we talk, we must explain things clearly. Even then, we fear that oral agreements are not binding; therefore, we draw up written contracts to which we sign our names. Laws arise in just this fash-

---

5. Emile Durkheim, *The Division of Labor in Society*, trans. George Simpson (New York: Free Press, 1964). In the original, Fei mistakenly inverts the two, equating *Gemeinschaft* with organic solidarity and *Gesellschaft* with mechanical solidarity. We have corrected the error in the translation.

ion. But there is no way for laws like this to develop in a rural society. "Isn't that what outsiders do?" rural people would say. In rural society, trust derives from familiarity. This kind of trust has very solid foundations, for it is rooted in customary norms. Even today, Western merchants often remark that trustworthiness is an innate quality of the Chinese. Many stories sound like fairy tales, such as the one told recently about a Westerner who received, after the war, a whole set of porcelain that his grandfather had ordered years earlier when he was in China. The goods were delivered without any charge and with the seller's profuse apologies for being unable to send them earlier. Trust in rural society is based not on the importance of contracts but, rather, on the dependability of people, people who are so enmeshed in customary norms that they cannot behave in any other way.

This sort of familiarity is a distinctive characteristic of being rural, of being a "hayseed," if you will. Only those who depend on the soil for their livelihood would root themselves in one place like a plant. Over time, people rooted in the same small place come to know everybody's life just as a mother knows her children. Strangers cannot understand what a baby says, but a mother not only clearly understands everything that her baby says, but she also understands what the baby wants even though the baby does not use words.

Rural people not only know each other intimately; they also get to know other aspects of rural life equally well. If an old farmer sees ants moving their anthill, he will quickly dig ditches in the fields, because he knows the meaning behind their move. Knowledge acquired from familiarity is specific and is not deduced from abstract general principles. People who grow up in a familiar environment do not need such principles. They only need to know the specific relationship between means and ends within the scope of their activities. They do not seek universal truths. When I read the *Analects,* I noticed that Confucius gave different definitions of filial piety *(xiao)* to different people. I realized then the special character of rural society. What is filial piety? Confucius did not give an abstract explanation, but gave different answers to different students by describing concrete behavioral examples. Finally, he concluded that filial piety is simply a peaceful mind. Sons and daughters should become thoroughly familiar with their parents' personalities in the course of daily contact, and then should try to please them in order to achieve peace of mind. The basic methods of human interaction in rural society rest on familiarity and on maintaining a peaceful mind.

These methods cannot be used with a stranger. China is undergoing a rapid transformation that is changing a fundamentally rural society into a modern one. The way of life that has been cultivated in rural society is now giving rise to abuses. Created by strangers, modern society cannot incorporate the customary basis of rural society. Rejecting the customary ways of rural life, modern people denigrate everything rural. The rural village is no longer a place to which successful people want to return.

2

Bringing Literacy to the Countryside

In the eyes of those living in cities, country people are "stupid" (*yu*). Even those people who advocate rural work regard stupidity, sickness, and poverty as symptoms of everything that is wrong in Chinese rural villages.[1] We can, of course, objectively measure sickness and poverty, but on what grounds can we say that country people are "stupid"? When peasants, walking in the middle of a road, hear a car honking behind them, they become so nervous that they simply do not know which way to jump. Then the drivers of those cars slam on the brakes, stick their heads out of the window, spit and curse, and call those peasants "stupid"! If that is stupidity, then country people have been wronged.

Once I took my students on a field trip to the countryside. After inspecting *corn* growing in one of the fields, a young female student, acting as if she knew it all, announced, "This year's *wheat* has grown extremely tall." The peasant standing beside her did not spit at her even once, but gave her a little smile, which an astute observer might have interpreted as a reaction to her stupidity. Country people do not know how to deal with traffic because they have never experienced how to live in a city. That is a question of knowledge, not of intelligence. In the same way, when city people visit the countryside, they do not even know something as simple as how to chase the dogs away; but we should not call them "idiots" just because they are frightened by barking dogs. By equal measure, we certainly have no reason to call country people "stu-

1. In this passage, where Fei addresses "those people who advocate rural work," he is referring to the intellectuals who led the Rural Reconstruction Movement. The leaders of this movement strongly advocated rural education and other measures to reform the countryside. It was a movement that Fei criticized a number of times. See R. David Arkush, *Fei Xiaotong and Sociology in Revolutionary China* (Cambridge, Mass.: Harvard University Press, 1981), pp. 37, 353.

pid" because they lack knowledge about such simple rules of the road as whether to walk on the left or on the right side. Stupidity has no bearing here.

When our well-meaning social workers say that country people are stupid, they usually mean that country people cannot read. They are illiterate, or what we call "character blind." Their eyes cannot even recognize one Chinese character. That they are illiterate is a fact. I would never oppose a movement to bring literacy to the countryside. However, it would be hard to convince me that illiteracy equals stupidity. "Stupidity" indicates a lack of, or a defect in, intelligence. The ability to read is not a measure of intelligence. Intelligence is the ability to learn. If people have had no opportunity to study, they will necessarily know very little, regardless of whether or not they possess the ability to learn. Therefore, do we mean to say that country people are not only illiterate but also incapable of learning?

During the war, when my colleagues and I were evacuated to a distant rural area, some of our children attended a rural elementary school. In whatever classes they attended, our children learned faster and had better grades than the country children. In front of all the parents, the teachers always praised our children as being bright and spirited, by which they meant that the children of professors naturally possess high intelligence. I was, of course, delighted with such compliments for my own child. For us poor professors, who had been deprived of nearly everything, it seemed nice that we could still bequeath to our children a natural ability that left others far behind. One day, however, I saw students catching grasshoppers in the field after school. Those "bright and spirited" children of ours chased those grasshoppers all over the place, but they failed to catch anything. At the same time, being very agile, the peasant children caught grasshoppers with every grab. On my way home, I felt my pride deflate.

That peasant children could not learn characters in the classroom faster than the professors' children is just like the fact that professors' children could not catch more grasshoppers than the peasant children. I did not blame my child for being unable to catch grasshoppers. First, our family did not need grasshoppers to supplement our food. In those rural areas of Yunnan, people like to add grasshoppers to their dishes; their taste is somewhat like the dried shrimps from Suzhou. Second, my child never had the opportunity to practice catching grasshoppers. Professors' children always wore socks and shoes. To keep their dignity, they had to walk very carefully, and if they got dirty, their parents would scold them. Therefore, even when they went after the grasshoppers, they would always have misgivings about it, and so would never be quite agile enough to catch them. These are probably the immediate reasons, but an even more basic reason is that they never ran wild in the fields every day; they never learned to distinguish a blade of grass from an insect. As a result of protective coloration, grasshoppers are always the same color as the grass, so it takes trained eyes to see them.

Can this reasoning that I just applied to my own child also be applied to rural children to explain their "stupidity" in learning characters? I think it fits perfectly. Unlike professors' children, those children from the countryside did not grow up seeing books and characters everywhere. That was not their daily fare. Professors' children did not inherit some special ability to learn characters well, but they obviously grew up in an environment that made learning characters easier. Therefore, seen in this fashion, the question about whether country people are the equals of city people in intelligence cannot be resolved.

When those social workers say that country people are stupid, they probably mean that their knowledge, and not their intelligence, is inferior. However, even this point seems implausible. At most, we can say that country people do not match city dwellers in their knowledge about what is required for city living. That much is correct. But can we not also say that there are many illiterate people in the countryside because life there does not require literacy? Now we arrive at a key point: What is the use of a written language?

In the last chapter, I showed that one of the characteristics of rural society is that people grow up among close acquaintances. In other words, people who work together see each other every single day. In sociology, we call this kind of group a "face-to-face" *(mianduimian)* group. Gui Youguang says in his book *Xiangjixuan ji* that, when he meets the same people every day, after a while he is able to tell who is coming by the sound of that person's footsteps.[2] In face-to-face groups, people can identify a visitor without actually seeing him. Although we have lived in modern cities for some time now, we have not completely given up those habits that are so prominent in rural society. Give this a try. The next time someone knocks on your door, just say, "Who is it?" I bet that the person behind the door will simply answer, in a loud voice, "Me!" You recognize the person by the voice. People who live in face-to-face groups do not need to say names. Would a wife say her name to answer her husband's question "Who is it?" We have become so accustomed to giving this "me" answer that sometimes we even do it when the person behind the door cannot recognize our voice. Once, when I returned to my hometown after a long absence, I remember answering a phone call. I had no way to identify the person on the other end of the line, who would only say, when I asked who was speaking, "It's me." I ended up making a blunder.

We ask for the name because we do not know the person. But this is not the way among people who are familiar with each other. Footsteps, voices, even smells are enough for identification. Even in our own social circles, we often omit names when we address one another. This shows that we, too, live among familiar people, and thus we duplicate, in some small degree, a rural society.

Before written languages came into existence, people tied knots in ropes to record things. They did so in order to overcome the difficulty in communicating across time and space. Only when we cannot talk face to face do we need something to replace the spoken word. In Guangxi province, in the mountains where the Yao minority lives, tribal groups notify each other about emergencies by sending runners who carry special coins. Upon receiving the coins, the other tribes will come to the rescue immediately. The coin here is a "character," a sign representing certain meanings upon which both parties previously agreed. If talking face to face is possible, however, such a sign not only would be unnecessary but also could cause misunderstandings. Before the last decade,

2. Gui Youguang was a scholar who lived during the Ming dynasty (1368–1644). The book *Xiangjixuan ji*, titled after Gui's name for his study, is a collection of his essays.

young lovers were prohibited from seeing each other.[3] In order to communicate, they exchanged love letters. Many tragedies were caused by misunderstandings in those love letters. People who have experienced such misunderstandings know all too well the limits of written language.

Written language cannot fully express one's meaning or emotion, because those meanings and emotions are always grounded in time and space; they fit a context. When one reads the written word, however, one is in a different time and probably in a different place; it is very unlikely that the meanings and emotions, so carefully recorded in written language, can be fully understood in that new context. As a tool for expressing oneself, written language has this irreparable flaw. Therefore, when we use written language, we must pay close attention to grammar, style, and syntax, because they help to lessen the misrepresentations inherent in written language.

When talking, we do not need to pay such close attention to grammar. I am not saying that there is no grammar in conversations but, rather, that when we talk, we also use many additional gestures to clarify what we say. We may point at ourselves while omitting the word "I," but we cannot do this when we write. Instead, we have to try our best to write grammatically correct sentences, because incorrect sentences may cause unfortunate misunderstandings. By contrast, when we use complete, grammatically correct sentences in speech, we sound funny and pedantic. This is the sort of painfully correct speech that one hears from people who learned a foreign language only from books.

Written language is indirect talk. It is an imperfect tool—so much so that telephones and broadcasting are already beginning to displace letters and other forms of writing. What will happen to the written word in the future, after still more developments in communication technology?

If we follow this line of reasoning, then, illiteracy cannot be equated with stupidity. Face-to-face communication is direct contact. Why should people in rural society abandon what is in that

3. Fei is referring to the tradition of arranged marriages. After the engagement had been announced, contact between the intended couple was forbidden. Often a bride would first meet her husband on the day of her wedding.

context a superior form of communication for one that does not serve as well?

Now I want to take the argument one step further.[4] In face-to-face groups, even spoken language is a tool, for which there is no alternative. Language is a symbolic system based on sounds. A symbol is a thing or an action to which meaning is attached. I say "attached" because "meaning" is not essential to the nature of the thing or the action but, rather, is something added through an association of ideas. A symbol is a social product that arises within the process of social interaction and that people use only as a way to convey meaning to others. Moreover, a symbol only functions as a symbol when other people recognize the meaning that was originally intended. A "meaningful" action, then, will result in the same response from most people. Thus, we can never have a strictly individual language, only social languages. To have the same meaning for the same symbol, people must have had the same experience; they must have been exposed to the same symbol in a similar environment, so that the same meaning can be attached to that symbol. This is the reason that every living group has its own special language, which contains many untranslatable words and sentences.

Language can occur only in the context of a group's common experience. In large groups, people's experiences are complex and often disconnected. They have fewer common experiences on which to base their language. Therefore, the larger the group, the more generalizable and simple the common language becomes—as can be clearly seen in the history of languages.

Besides a common language that the group as a whole shares, there will also be, within the same group, many specialized vocabularies used by various subgroups to articulate their special requirements. Such "working languages" are filled with jargon and idioms. People in the same profession typically have a language of the trade. Other people cannot understand the conversations, be-

4. Fei's argument at this point seems to draw heavily on the social psychology of George Herbert Mead, whose writings were influential in the Chicago school of sociology. Fei likely learned about this group from Robert Park in China and from travels in the United States. For more on this perspective, see George Herbert Mead, *Mind, Self, and Society* (Chicago: University of Chicago Press, 1934). We should note that Fei advances this perspective by making an especially nice contrast between written and spoken languages.

cause they have not shared the same working experience. In every school and even every dormitory room, specialized vocabularies develop. The most widely occurring "working language" is that which develops between mothers and their children.

Such working languages are only one aspect of the system of symbols used by tightly knit groups. This is the part that is based on sound and that can be verbalized. In such groups, however, many nonverbal symbols can also be used. Facial expressions and gestures are sometimes more expressive than sound in face-to-face settings. Even when a verbal language is used, it is always used in the context of other symbols. I might say to an acquaintance, "That's the way it is." At the same time, I would frown, tighten my lips, rub my temples, and lower my head. The person would understand that the phrase means "It can't be helped" and would sense my disappointment. If the same phrase is used with a different expression, its meaning is entirely different.

Working languages are usually very effective, because they loosen the fixed meanings of words. Language is society's sifter. Those feelings and meanings that differ in size and shape from the holes in the sifter cannot pass through the sifter. I am sure that everyone must have experienced a time when silence really is "better than words." It is in fact true that, although this social sifter helps people understand each other, it also formalizes their meanings and their emotions. In this way, language distorts actual meanings and emotions the very moment they are articulated through words. We always trim the toes to fit the shoes. Language constrains what can be felt and expressed, and sensitive people often resent that.

In face-to-face groups, we speak less. We convey our intentions with our eyes, our emotions with a gesture. We abandon indirect symbols to seek more direct understandings. That is why written language is superfluous in rural society, and even spoken language is not the only way to communicate symbolically.

I absolutely do not mean to suggest that we need not promote literacy in the countryside. With the process of modernization, rural society is already being changed, and literacy is the tool of that change. The point I want to make here is that illiteracy in the countryside results not from people's stupidity but, rather, from the nature of rural society itself. I would like to go even further to say that one should not judge the degree of understanding between people in a society only from the perspective of their written and spoken languages. This is not enough. Written and spoken languages are tools for expression, but they are not the only tools. Moreover, the tools themselves have flaws and limit what can be conveyed. Those advocates of rural literacy should first consider the social foundation of both written and spoken languages. Otherwise, just opening a few rural schools and teaching rural people a few characters will not create "intelligence," as the advocates define it.

3

More Thoughts on
Bringing Literacy to the Countryside

In the last chapter, I said that written language develops when time and space put limits on direct human communication. I only discussed, however, how space influences this development. In rural society, which is a face-to-face society, people can talk directly to one another and do not need to rely on a written language. But how does separation across time influence the process of human communication?

There are two aspects of this question that we need to discuss. First is the spread of time over a person's lifetime, and the second is the spread of time across generations. Let me begin with the first aspect.

What differentiates human beings from other animals is the extraordinary ability of humans to learn.[1] Most forms of human behavior are not predetermined by innate physiological reactions. What we mean by learning is exactly that process by which human beings, from the time of their birth, reshape their instincts, making them fit man-made behavioral molds. This shaping of behavior is accomplished through "practice." Practice means "training," doing the same thing again and again until a new routine becomes thoroughly ingrained. Therefore, for the individual, learning necessarily breaks down the separation between the past and the present. Human beings have that special ability, which we call "memory," that bridges time. To be sure, animals also have memories, but their memories operate only at a simple physiological level. A white mouse learns which is the shortest route in a maze, but what the mouse learns is merely a new set of physiological reactions. That

1. In making this distinction between human and animal communication, Fei follows the thesis developed by George Herbert Mead in *Mind, Self, and Society* (Chicago: University of Chicago Press, 1934), pp. 42–60. More recent research has shown that this distinction is less clear-cut than Mead or Fei suggested.

kind of learning does not depend on a symbolic system. Humans certainly have many habits that are basic to human nature, and in this regard they are like mice running in a maze. But unlike mice, humans are always helped along by their symbolic system of communication, and the most important elements of this system are words. We learn through talking. We abstract the concrete world. We express our reality by a set of concepts that can be applied universally. Such concepts are necessarily expressed through words; by relying on words, we move from the specific to the universal. Concepts create the bridge that joins one event with another. Concepts allow us to move backward into the past as well as forward into the future; concepts allow us to bridge time. From this perspective, animals relate to time in a direct way: stimulus, then response. The human relation to time, however, is mediated through concepts. Words make the world more complex to humans than it is to animals. By simply closing their eyes, humans can envision their past, and from that past, from that accumulation of events and ideas, they can selectively draw out the images needed to interpret the present.

Animals, living instinctively, do not have a problem with time. Their lives form a chain of presents. No one can stop time, just as no knife can cut off the flow of water. But human time differs from animal time. The human present is the total accumulation of the past that is retained through memory. If we lost our memory, our recognition of time would cease.

Humans have such a memory not because their brains operate automatically, like cameras. Humans have the ability to remember, it is true. But they utilize and develop this ability because their present lives must necessarily include ways of doing things that have been transmitted from the past. I already have said that humans learn by incorporating into their behavior preexisting patterns. Only when they have learned these patterns are they able to live in groups. These patterns are not each person's individual creation; they are the legacy of society. The white mouse does not learn from other mice. In order to adapt to its own environment, each mouse has to acquire its own set of experiences through a process of trial and error. Mice are unable to transmit their experiences to other mice; they cannot learn from each other. Humans, however, have the ability to think abstractly and to use complex symbols. They can accumulate not only their own experiences but also those of others. The transmitted patterns are the accumulations of a group's common experiences, which we often refer to by the term *culture*. Culture is the collective social experience perpetuated by a symbolic system and individual memories. In this way, each person's "present" contains not only the projection of his or her own past but also that of the whole group's past. For individuals, history is not mere ornamentation but the very foundation of life; it is both practical and indispensable. Humans must live in groups; they must learn culture; but to learn culture requires memory, not instincts. Therefore, humans have had to cultivate their ability to remember. They use this ability not only to bridge their own past and present but also to bridge generations, for without this ability there would be neither culture nor the life that we now enjoy.

Perhaps I have said enough on this topic to demonstrate the connection between human life and time. This connection rests upon the ability to use words. It has been said that the language makes the people, and I think this is absolutely correct. The Bible, you will recall, says that when God said something, that something immediately came into existence.[2] Saying is the beginning of being—if not in the material world, certainly in the cultural world. Without a symbolic system, there would be no concepts. And without concepts, there would be no accumulation of human experiences across time. Human life could not go beyond that of animals.

Writing employs symbols that can be recognized by the human eye, but words do not need to be written in order to be symbols. Words can be spoken. Every culture has "words," but not all cultures have a written language. I emphasize this point because I want to show that, generally speaking, rural society is a society without a written language. In the last chapter, I showed that country people do not need to use a written language because they are not separated in space. Now I want to show the same result for their relationship with time.

2. Fei's reference is to the biblical story of creation from Genesis, chap. 1.

I just said that we have developed our capacity for memory because our lives require it. Animals, being without culture, manage their lives through instincts, so they have no need for memory. What I have said actually implies something else as well. The requirements for human living determine the level to which our memory actually develops. The world that we encounter at every moment is very complex; we do not take all of it in through our senses. We are selective. Our line of vision moves with the shifting focus of our attention, and our choice of focus depends on the meanings objects have for our livelihood. Those things having no relevance in our lives go unnoticed. Our memory works in the same way. It does not record everything that occurs in the past, but only a small part of it. Actually, it is more accurate to say "recall" than "record." "Record" suggests that we note something in the present for use in the future. "Recall," however, means that we reflect back on our past experience to establish a connection to the present. In fact, it is very difficult to foresee in the present what might be useful in the future. Instead, what we need in the present is constructed selectively by our recalling of the past. This process can sometimes be very hard, as with the so-called painful recall. In any event, our memory is never useless; it is practical, for out of it comes the ability to live as humans.

The range of memory needed by a person living in rural society is not the same as that required for one living in modern cities. Life in rural society is very stable. I have said that people who make their living from the earth cannot readily move. The place of their birth is the place where they grow up and where they die. The most extreme version of this rural model is Laotse's ideal society, where, "although they can hear their neighbors' chickens and dogs, people grow and die without ever visiting their neighbors."[3] In truth, not only do people rarely leave their hometown, but their hometown is usually the same as that of their parents. This is the consequence of being born and dying in the same place. Even though this extreme version of rural society is seldom realized, people often do intend to stay in one place forever. Otherwise, why should people who have died in other places request in their will to have their coffin transported back to their hometown for burial in the family

3. Laotse, *Dao de jing*, chap. 80.

graveyard?[4] They have taken their life from this piece of soil, so after death they want to return their flesh and bones to it.

Because people seldom move, they grow up not only among familiar people but also in familiar places. Staying in the same place for such a long time, the people there seem to intermingle with the earth itself. The experiences of one's ancestors with this familiar patch of earth are passed down and necessarily become one's own experiences. The ages speak as if their lessons were written in stone. These lessons surround ensuing generations and are repeated endlessly, so that each person's experiences are the same as every other person's. It is like a play repeated on the stage; actors need only to remember the same set of lines. Each person's individual experience equals that of the entire generation. There is no need to accumulate experience, only to preserve it as it is.

I remember that, when I was in elementary school, a teacher forced us to keep a diary. Although I took great pains to think about what I did, it seemed, after a while, that I only wrote the same line: "The same as above." And that was true, too. Every day my life was the same. Get up in the morning, go to school, play, and go to sleep at night. What else could I write? When the teacher forbade all the students to write "The same as above," we had to make up lies.

When the patterns of life are fixed on physiological habits, our existence takes on a working rhythm: "Wake with the sun and rest with the dusk." Memory becomes superfluous. The saying "We act as if we never know that old age is coming" *(bu zhi lao zhi jiang zhi)* describes a life in which we forget time. The fall of the Qin, the rise of the Han—what difference does it make?[5] People in rural society do not fear forgetfulness. They are even quite comfortable with it.

Only when we want to remember to do something outside our normal routine do we tie a knot around our finger. That string on our finger is a primitive form of written language. Such a language

---

4. The practice of returning the corpse to the lineage burial ground has been so widespread among migrating Chinese in traditional times that their migrant associations took this repatriation of bodies to be one of their chief rationales for existence.

5. Qin (221–207 B.C.) and Han (206 B.C.–A.D. 220) are the names of the first two dynasties of the imperial period in Chinese history.

serves to assist human memory by means of external symbols that create an association among ideas. In a frequently changing environment, we sense that our memory may be inadequate, and so we need to use external symbols. At this point, language is transformed from a spoken language into a written language, from communication based on sounds to one based on words. Language becomes the ability to use a rope to tie knots, a knife to carve ideograms, a brush to write characters—all of which necessarily occur when our lives are changed from a fixed to an ever-changing existence. People who live in cities and see strange faces day in and day out need to keep an address book in their pockets. In rural society, even an identification card bearing a photograph is totally meaningless. There may be over a dozen "elder brother Wangs" in a village, but nobody would mistake one for another.

In a society where the life of each generation appears before us like a movie played over and over again, history is simply unnecessary. What is past is only a legend. Whenever people account for the origins of things, they begin with the same phrase, "When heaven separated from the earth." They have to begin, with a bang, at the exciting starting point, because what follows will be only ordinary things like those at present. In urban society, there is news; but in rural society, news is something strange and absurd. In urban society, there are celebrities; but in rural society, as the saying goes, "People fear becoming famous just as pigs fear becoming fat."[6] No one should lead, no one should follow. Everyone should be the same, and everyone should follow the same path. People in this kind of society do not distribute themselves in the form of a normal curve. Instead, all of them act as if they are made out of the same mold.

In this kind of society, a spoken language is sufficient to pass experience between generations. When a person has a problem, he or she is certain to get an effective solution from someone older. People all live in the same environment. They all walk along the same path, but some walk there earlier than others do. The ones who come later step into the footprints of those who walked ear-

6. The meaning of the phrase, which is not necessarily obvious to Westerners, is that, like pigs that are eaten when they grow fat, celebrities draw the attention of people who will try to take advantage of them and lead them and their families to ruin.

lier. Experience of this sort can be passed from mouth to mouth without anything being lost. So where is the need for a written language? Time provides no obstacle; one thing closely follows another. An entire culture can be passed between fathers and sons without any omissions.

This being the case, if China is a rural society, how could a written language have come into existence in the first place? My answer is that, although the foundation of Chinese society is certainly rural, Chinese writing itself did not develop in rural society. The earliest characters had a religious quality to them and were used in temples; those characters, even down to the present time, have never belonged to the people in the countryside. Our written language emerged in a different setting. In this chapter, all that I want to point out is that, at the most basic level, at the rural level, there is spoken language but no genuine use for a written language. If we consider the spatial and temporal qualities of rural life, we must conclude that country people live their lives in face-to-face intimacy and with repetitious and rigid life patterns. Rural people are certainly not too stupid to learn characters. Instead, they have no need for characters to assist them, because a written language does not help them with the necessities of living in rural society. If China's rural foundations were to change, then—and perhaps only then—literacy would come to the countryside.

4

Chaxugeju:
The Differential Mode of Association

Selfishness is the most serious shortcoming of country people. That is the opinion of those intellectuals who advocate rural reconstruction.[1] When we think of selfishness, we think of the proverb "Each person should sweep the snow from his own doorsteps and should not fret about the frost on his neighbor's roof." No one would deny that this proverb is one of the Chinese creeds. Actually, this attitude is held not only by country people but also by city people. The person who only sweeps the snow from his own door is still regarded as having high social ethics.

Ordinary people usually throw their garbage onto the streets right in front of their door, and that is the end of their garbage problem. For instance, in Suzhou the houses usually have back doors that open onto slow-moving canals. This sounds very beautiful, and, in fact, literary works depict Suzhou as the Chinese Venice. But I do not think that there are any waterways in the world dirtier than those in Suzhou. Everything can be thrown into the canals, which even in the best of circumstances do not flow well. Filled with garbage, they flow even worse. Many families use no other toilets. Even knowing full well that other people wash clothes and vegetables in the canals, they feel no need for self-restraint.

Why is this so? The reason is that such canals belong to the public. Once you mention something as belonging to the public, it is almost like saying that everyone can take advantage of it. Thus, one can have rights without obligations. Even if we reduce the scale and look at a small courtyard shared by two or three families, we can still see dirt piled in the public corridors and weeds growing in the backyard. No one wants to clean or to weed. But the

---

1. See chapter 2, note 1.

worst place in such a courtyard would be the public toilets. Not a single family wants to take care of this business. Whoever finds the condition of the toilet intolerable has to clean it up without pay or even without thanks. It is like Gresham's law. Just as "bad money drives out the good," selfishness drives out social consciousness.

Judging from examples like this, the problem of selfishness in China is really more common than the problem of ignorance or illness. From the top of society to the bottom, no one seems to be without this shortcoming. It has, in fact, gained some notoriety. Corruption and incompetence have become a stereotype of Chinese people that the foreign media use to belittle us. But so-called corruption and incompetence have less to do with individual ability than with each person's service to, and responsibility for, the public welfare.

The Chinese are not bad managers. Indeed, a great many Westerners are impressed by the business achievements of the overseas Chinese in Southeast Asia. Neither are the Chinese incompetent. When it comes to managing their family's businesses, earning money, and making personal connections, they show a greater aptitude than people from any other country. The problem defined by this kind of selfishness is thus actually one of how to draw the line between the group and the individual, between others and our own selves. How this line has been drawn in China traditionally is obviously different from the way it is drawn in the West. Therefore, if we want to discuss the problem of selfishness, we have to take into consideration the pattern of the entire social structure.

Western societies are somewhat like the way we collect rice straw to use to cook our food. After harvest, the rice straw is bound into small bundles; several bundles are bound into larger bundles; and these are then stacked together so that they can be carried on shoulder poles. Each piece of straw belongs in a small bundle, which in turn belongs in a larger bundle, which in turn makes up a stack. The separate straws, the separate bundles, and finally the separate stacks all fit together to make up the whole haystack. In this way, the separately bound bundles can be stacked in an orderly way.

In Western society, these separate units are organizations. By making an analogy between organizations in Western societies and the composition of haystacks, I want to indicate that in Western society individuals form organizations. Each organization has its own boundaries, which clearly define those people who are members and those who are not. That much is always clear. The people in an organization form a group, and their relationship to the organization is usually the same. If there are differences among group members or distinctions among ranks within the organization, these would have been agreed upon earlier as part of the rules of the organization.

In one respect, my analogy is not too appropriate. An individual may join several organizations, but it is impossible for a straw to be in several bundles at the same time. That is the difference between people and straws. My purpose in making the analogy, however, is only to help us see more concretely the pattern of personal relationships in social life, what I will henceforth call the "organizational mode of association" *(tuantigeju)*.

Families in the West are organizations with distinct boundaries. If a Western friend writes to you saying that he will "bring his family" to visit you, you know very well who will be coming with him. In China, however, this sentence is very ambiguous. In England and America, a family will include the man, his wife, and his children who have not yet grown up. If he is bringing only his wife, he does not use the word *family*. In China, we often see the sentence "The whole family will come" *(hedi guanglin)*, but few people can tell what family members should be included in the word *di* (family). In Chinese, the word *jia* (family) is used in many ways. *Jialide* (the one at home) can mean one's wife. *Jiamen* (kinsmen) may be directed at a big group of uncles and nephews. *Zijiaren* (my own people) may include anyone whom you want to drag into your own circle, and you use it to indicate your intimacy with them. The scope of *zijiaren* can be expanded or contracted according to the specific time and place. It can be used in a very general way, even to mean that everyone under the sun is a *jia* (one family).

Why are nouns for such basic social units so ambiguous in Chinese? In my opinion, the ambiguity indicates the difference between our social structure and that of the West. Our pattern is not like distinct bundles of straws. Rather, it is like the circles that appear on the surface of a lake when a rock is thrown into it. Everyone stands at the center of the circles produced by his or her own social influence. Everyone's circles are interrelated. One touches different circles at different times and places.

In Chinese society, the most important relationship—kinship—is similar to the concentric circles formed when a stone is thrown into a lake. Kinship is a social relationship formed through marriage and reproduction. The networks woven by marriage and reproduction can be extended to embrace countless numbers of people—in the past, present, and future. The same meaning is implied in our saying "Everyone has a cousin three thousand miles away," with three thousand miles indicating the vastness of kinship networks. Despite the vastness, though, each network is like a spider's web in the sense that it centers on oneself. Everyone has this kind of a kinship network, but the people covered by one network are not the same as those covered by any other. We all use the same system of notation to identify our relatives, but the only thing we hold in common is the system of notation itself. This system is merely an abstract pattern, a set of categorical concepts. When we use this system to identify concrete relatives, however, each term identifies a different person. In our kinship system, we all have parents, but my parents are not your parents. No two people in the world can have entirely the same set of relatives. Two brothers certainly would have the same parents, but each brother would have his own wife and children. Therefore, the web of social relationships linked with kinship is specific to each person. Each web has a self as its center, and every web has a different center.

In our rural society, this pattern of organization applies not only to kinship but also to spatial relationships. An exception might be the modern *baojia* system, which is somewhat similar to the Western organizational mode of association *(tuantigeju)* and is quite incompatible with traditional social structure.[2] In the traditional

2. *Baojia* is a system of local control, instituted in several forms during the imperial period. The system was based on mutual responsibility of households. Local populations were divided into units, usually composed of ten households each. Members would mutually have the responsibility of seeing that everyone in the *baojia* unit maintained good order. If a violation occurred and caught the attention of officials, everyone in the *baojia* unit would be punished for the crime of one of its members. For Fei's discussion of the *baojia* system that was instituted during the Republican period, see *Xiangtu chongjian* (Reconstructing rural China) (Xianggang: Wenxue chubanshe, n.d.), chap. 4, p. 50.

structure, every family regards its own household as the center and draws a circle around it. This circle is the neighborhood, which is established to facilitate reciprocation in daily life. A family invites the neighbors to its weddings, sends them red-dyed eggs when a new baby is born, and asks for their help in lifting its dead into coffins and carrying the coffins to the cemetery. But a neighborhood is not a fixed group. Instead, it is an area whose size is determined by the power and authority of each center. The neighborhood of a powerful family may expand to the entire village, while a poor family's neighborhood is composed of only two or three nearby families.

This pattern is just like the circles of kinship. For instance, in *The Dream of the Red Chamber*, the story's main family, the Jia family, was so wealthy and powerful that the family's compound contained both Lin Daiyu, a cousin on the father's side, and Xue Baochai, a cousin on the mother's side.[3] Later in the story, the Jia family house, which was called "Jia's Grand Garden," contained even more distant relatives, such as Baoqin and Xiuyun. But when the Jia family lost its power and wealth, the family dwindled away into a tiny group. As the saying goes, "When the tree falls, the monkeys scatter." There is even a more extreme case, that of Su Qin, who, after seeking his fortune for many years, returned home as a total failure.[4] His wife refused to regard him as a husband, and his sister-in-law refused to regard him as her brother-in-law.

This pattern of organization in Chinese traditional society has the special quality of elasticity. In the country, families can be very small, but in the wealthy landlord and bureaucratic classes, families can be as big as small kingdoms. These highly elastic social circles, which can be expanded or contracted according to a change in the power of the center, cause the Chinese to be particularly sensitive to changes in human relationships.

In the West, everyone recognizes his or her social boundaries. Even adult children who still live with their parents usually pay for

3. Written in the eighteenth century by Cao Xueqin, *The Dream of the Red Chamber*, also known as *The Story of the Stone*, is China's most famous and widely read novel. The translation by David Hawkes is the best and most complete: Cao Xueqin, *The Story of the Stone* (5 vols.) (Middlesex, England: Penguin Books, 1973).

4. Su Qin, whose story is recounted in Sima Qian's *Shiji* (The book of history), lived during the Warring States period (480–221 B.C.). Su Qin was renowned for his political intrigues and was eventually executed for spying.

their room and board. People in an organization must fulfill the particular qualifications for membership, and, accordingly, people who no longer possess those qualifications must leave the organization. To Westerners, such requirements show not a lack of human warmth but, rather, a respect for individual rights. Westerners struggle for their rights, but in our society people seek connections in higher places and do things for the sake of friendship.

According to the Western pattern, all members in an organization are equivalent, just as all straws in a bundle are alike. This is quite different from the Chinese pattern. Social relationships in China possess a self-centered quality. Like the ripples formed from a stone thrown into a lake, each circle spreading out from the center becomes more distant and at the same time more insignificant. With this pattern, we are faced with the basic characteristic of Chinese social structure, or what the Confucian school has called *renlun* (human relationships). What is *lun*? To me, insofar as it is used to describe Chinese social relationships, the term itself signifies the ripplelike effect created from circles of relationships that spread out from the self, an effect that produces a pattern of discrete circles. In the ancient text *Shiming* (The interpretation of names), *lun* is defined as "the order existing in ripples of water." Pan Guangdan once said, "Word combinations with *lun* all have similar meanings, which express proper arrangements, classifications, and order."[5]

Lun stresses differentiation. In the *Book of Rites* (*Liji*), the "ten relationships" form a discontinuous classification. Gods and ghosts, monarchs and subjects, fathers and sons, the noble and the base, the intimate and the unconnected, the rewarded and the punished, husbands and wives, public affairs and private affairs, seniors and juniors, and superiors and inferiors—these are principal types of human relationships. "Everyone should stay in his place" (*bu shi qi lun*); thereby, fathers are differentiated from sons, those remote from those close, those who are intimate from those who are not.[6]

5. Fei's note: Pan Guangdan, "Shuo lunzi" (On relationships), *Shehui yanjiu* (Social study), 19.
6. The *Book of Rites*, one of the Confucian classics, was compiled during the Western Han period (206 B.C.–A.D. 8) and contains early discussion of ritual practices.

Lun is order based on classifications. Some may wonder why the concrete social relationships, such as gods and ghosts, monarchs and subjects, fathers and sons, and husbands and wives, are placed in the same category as the abstract positional types, such as the noble and the base, the intimate and the unconnected, the remote and the close, those above and those below. In fact, the basic character of traditional Chinese social structure rests precisely on such hierarchical differentiations as these. Therefore, the key to understanding networks of human relationships is to recognize that such distinctions create the very patterns of Chinese social organization. In the *Book of Rites*, it is written, "Toward the intimate, there is only intimacy; toward the respected, only respect; toward superiors, only deference; between men and women, only differences; these are things that people cannot alter." This means that the framework of social structure is unchangeable; what is changeable is only the use to which the framework is put.

Confucius paid a lot of attention to the word *tui* (pushing or extending out), in the sense of ripples expanding out from the center. He first recognized the centrality of the self. Noting that one should "do to others as you would have done to yourself," Confucius explained that one should "control oneself and conform to rituals" (*ke ji fu li*). By exercising such self-restraint, one cultivates moral character. Attaining control over one's inner self, one then can *tui*, can extend oneself out into other circles of human relationships. Confucius wrote, "When the inner person is established, the way is born. . . . A man who is a good son and a dutiful brother will seldom be disposed to quarrel with those in authority over him, and a man who is not disposed to quarrel with those in authority will never be found to disturb the peace and order of the state. A gentleman devotes his attention to the fundamental principles of life. When this foundation is laid, wisdom will follow."[7] The path runs from the self to the family, from the family to the state, and from the state to the whole world (*tianxia*). In the *Doctrine of the Mean* (*Zhongyong*), the five relationships (monarch and

---

7. *Analects*, Book 1, chap. 2. The *Analects*, *The Works of Mencius*, *The Great Learning*, and the *Doctrine of the Mean* make up what is known in China as the "Four Books." These books were regarded as Confucian classics and constituted the core of classical education. The *Analects* contains a compilation of dialogues between Confucius and his disciples.

subject, father and son, husband and wife, older and younger brothers, and friends) are regarded as passages to the world (*tianxia zhi dadao*).[8] In such a social structure, the way to go beyond oneself and reach out to the world is to extend oneself circle by circle. Mencius even praised Confucius by saying that he "was good at extending himself."

In these elastic networks that make up Chinese society, there is always a self at the center of each web. But this notion of the self amounts to egocentrism, not individualism. With individualism, individuals make up organizations in the same way that parts make up the whole. The balance between parts and whole produces a concept of equality: since the position of each individual in an organization is the same, one person cannot encroach on the others. It also produces a concept of constitutionality: an organization cannot deny the rights of an individual; it controls individuals merely on the basis of the partial rights they have willingly handed over. Without these concepts, such organizations as these could not exist. However, in Chinese traditional thought, there is no comparable set of ideas, because, for us, there is only egocentrism. Everything worthwhile rests on an ideology in which the self is central.

This kind of egocentrism is not limited to the actions of someone like Yang Zhu, who was unwilling to pluck out even a single hair in order to benefit the world.[9] It also includes the Confucians. The difference between Yang Zhu and Confucius himself is that Yang Zhu neglected the relative, elastic qualities of egocentrism. He held his self close and would not let it out. Confucius, however, felt that people need to extend beyond themselves in order to achieve their own interests. But even if one extends as far as possible, one's self is still at the center. Confucius wrote, "A ruler who uses government to achieve virtue is like the North Star, which makes all the others stars surround it."[10] This is, in fact, a very apt simile for describing the Chinese system of organization, that of a pattern of

8. *Zhongyong* (Doctrine of the mean) is one of the four books regarded as the classic texts of Chinese civilization. It is said to have been written by Zisi in the Warring States period (480–221 B.C.).

9. Yang Zhu, a philosopher who lived in the Warring States period (480–221 B.C.), opposed the ethical philosophy of Confucius and Motzu and advocated the importance of individual life and self-interest.

10. *Analects*, Book 2, chap. 1.

discrete circles, the differential mode of association (*chaxugeju*). The self is always at the center; so, like the motionless North Star, the self is always surrounded by others who come under the influence of the center. In this regard, Confucius is not like Jesus Christ. Jesus transcends human organizations. He has his Heaven; so he can sacrifice himself for the sake of Heaven, for something beyond human society.

Confucius, however, is different. One of his disciples, Zigong, said to him, "If there were a man who extensively carried out good works for the welfare of the people and really gave benefits to the multitude, what would you say of such a man? Could he be called benevolent (*ren*)?" The Master said, "It is not a matter of benevolence with such a man. If you must describe him, sage is the right word. Even Yao and Shun would have found it difficult to accomplish as much. A benevolent man, in forming his own moral character, forms the character of others; in enlightening himself, he enlightens others. This is a good method for attaining a moral life, if one is able to profit by the example of those near at hand." [11]

Confucian ethics cannot be divorced from the idea of discrete centers fanning out into a weblike network. As Confucius wrote, "What the superior man seeks is in himself; what the petty man seeks is in others." With sentiments such as these, Confucius could not be like Jesus, who so loved everyone under the sun, including his enemies, that he asked God to have mercy on those who killed him. These actions could not have been motivated by egocentrism. What would Confucius have done? When someone asked him, "What about returning good for evil?" Confucius answered, "Why should one return good for evil? Treat evil with justice and return good for good." [12] Confucius could not put aside these kinds of distinctions. But Confucius was certainly not like Yang Zhu, who used his miserly little self to control all situations. Instead, Confucius expanded and contracted the moral scope according to necessity.

Once we understand these highly elastic social spheres, we are able to understand the problem of selfishness in Chinese soci-

---

11. Ibid., Book 6, chap. 28. Yao and Shun are the legendary early rulers of China who established China's golden age.
12. Ibid., Book 14, chap. 36.

ety. I often think that the Chinese would sacrifice their families for their own self-interests, their party for their families' interests, their country for their party's interests, and the whole world for their country's interests. This same idea is found in the classic book *The Great Learning*: "The ancients who wished to display illustrious virtue throughout the empire first put their own states in good order. Wishing to order their states, they first regulated their families. Wishing to regulate their families, they first cultivated their own self. Their self being cultivated, their families were regulated; their families being regulated, their states were correctly governed. Their states being well governed, the whole empire was made tranquil and peaceful.[13]

Now we can see that the boundary between the public and private spheres is relative—we may even say ambiguous. In *The Great Learning*, public order is achieved by moving toward the center of the discrete circles—that is, toward the family. Private selfishness, however, is justified by moving outward, toward the state. Both public officials and private persons use the same ambiguous conception of the social order to define the context of their action. This situation differs greatly from that in Western society, in which public and private rights and obligations are divided distinctly.

Sacrificing the family for one's own interests, or the lineage for the interests of one's household, is in reality a formula. With this formula, it is impossible to prove that someone is acting selfishly. The person concerned would likely deny it. He might contend that a person who sacrifices his lineage for the sake of his family is performing a public duty. When he sacrifices his country in struggling for the interests and rights of his own small group, he is still acting on behalf of the public, which is now defined as the small group itself. In this pattern of oscillating but differential social circles (*chaxugeju*), public and private are relative concepts. Standing in any circle, one can say that all those in that circle are part of the public. As a matter of fact, when Western diplomats work for the benefit of their own countries in international conferences, they willingly sacrifice world peace and other countries' legal rights; these actions are the same as ours. But the difference is that Westerners

13. *The Great Learning*, sec. 4. This book is included among the four great books of Chinese civilization. Its authorship is unclear.

regard the state as an organization surpassing all smaller groups. Both international and local affairs can be sacrificed for the sake of the state, but the state cannot be sacrificed for other groups. This is the concept of the modern state. It is a concept absent from Chinese rural society.

In the West, the state is an organization that creates distinct boundaries between the public and the private spheres. Like straws in a haystack, citizens all belong to the state. They have to make the state a public organization beneficial to each individual. Therefore, they have revolutions, constitutions, laws, and parliamentary bodies. But in traditional China, the concept of public was the ambiguous *tianxia* (all under heaven), whereas the state was seen as the emperor's family. Hence, the boundary between public and private has never been clear. The state and the public are but additional circles that spread out like the waves from the splash of each person's social influence. Therefore, people must cultivate themselves before they can extend outward. Accordingly, self-restraint has become the most important virtue in social life. The Chinese thus are unable to assert themselves against society to ensure that society does not infringe on their individual rights. In fact, the Chinese notion of a differential mode of association (*chaxugeju*) does not allow for individual rights to be an issue at all.

In the pattern of Chinese organization, our social relationships spread out gradually, from individual to individual, resulting in an accumulation of personal connections. These social relationships form a network composed of each individual's personal connections. Therefore, our social morality makes sense only in terms of these personal connections. I will discuss this last point in the next chapter.

5

The Morality of
Personal Relationships

The basic structure of Chinese rural society is what I have called "a differential mode of association" (*chaxugeju*). This pattern is composed of distinctive networks spreading out from each individual's personal connections. It is quite different from the modern Western organizational mode of association (*tuantigeju*). In such a pattern, personal relationships depend on a common structure. People attach themselves to a preexisting structure and then, through that structure, form personal relationships. The concept of the citizen, for example, necessarily follows the development of the state. It seems likely that this type of organizational pattern grew out of primitive tribal formations. In primitive nomadic economies, these patterns were quite prominent. Depending on each other in daily life, tribal peoples could not survive if they spread out among the mountains, with each person living alone. To them, a cohesive organization was a precondition of life. But it is different for those people living in a settled agricultural society, where everyone earns his or her own living from the land and feels the need of companions only under fortuitous, temporary, or special circumstances. To these people, starting relationships with others is a matter of secondary importance. Moreover, they need connections to different degrees on different occasions. They do not seem to need large, continuous organizations. Therefore, their society has adopted a differential mode of association.

These two patterns of social organization give rise to different types of morality. Morality is the belief that people in a society should abide by certain norms of social behavior. Morality always includes regulations, beliefs, and sanctions, all of which are shaped by the constraints imposed by a social structure. According to a sociological perspective, morality is society's sanction on individual behavior; it makes people conform to established social norms in order to maintain the existence and continuity of the society.

In the Western pattern, the fundamental concept of morality is built on the relationship between the organization and the individual. An organization is an entity that transcends the individual. Even so, organization itself has no material reality. It is impossible to call material things an organization. Instead, an organization is really a kind of social relationship among human beings. It is a force controlling individual behavior. It is an object on which the composition of individual elements depends. It is a common will that precedes individual members, even as it relies on them for its very existence.

The concept of organization can be expressed only by symbols. It is for this reason that the idea of an omnipresent God arose in the West. The relationship between the organization and the individual is signified in the relationship between God and his disciples. God is a judge who rewards and punishes, a keeper of justice who is an omnipotent protector.

If we want to understand the morality produced by Western organizational patterns, we must never leave out their religious concepts. Religious piety and beliefs are not only the source of Western morality but also the force that supports Western behavioral norms. From the concept of God, who is actually the symbol of universal organization, two important corollaries have emerged. One is that everyone is equal before God, and the other is that God treats everyone with equal justice.

Jesus addressed God as the Father, as everyone's Father. He even publicly rejected his own parents, who gave birth to him and brought him up. To achieve this equality, according to Christian beliefs, Jesus was born of a young virgin; the special and personal relationship between father and son is denied here. This denial is actually not nonsense; it is, instead, a powerful symbol of the public quality of organizations. God represents the universality of public organizations. God is necessarily without a private side. Jesus symbolizes each person within this universal organization. Besides a biological father, each person, therefore, shares a more important heavenly father—that is, an all-encompassing organization. Only by means of this conceptual thinking can the equality among individuals be established. The relationship of each member to the organization is the same. This organization cannot be any individual's private possession. These complex ideas are the very ones that form the basis of the American Declaration of Independence, whose main theme is clearly stated at the very beginning: "We hold these truths to be self-evident, that all men are created equal, that they are endowed by their creator with certain inalienable rights."

But God is not of this world. He symbolizes the invisible entity of universal organization. To carry out the will of organizations, ministers are needed. The term *minister* is a basic concept in the Western organizational mode of association. The person who carries out God's will is a minister, and the official who executes the power in an organization is also a minister. Both of them are agents. They are not gods themselves. Nor do they somehow embody the organization itself. The difference between God and his ministers, or between the state and its ministers, is never ambiguous. Throughout the history of Christianity, people have time and again tried to communicate with God directly and have opposed the agents on the grounds that they do not truly act at God's behest. Following the same logic, and in fact having grown out of it, the Declaration of Independence further states, "That to secure these rights, governments are instituted among men, deriving their just powers from the consent of the governed. That whenever any form of government becomes destructive of these ends, it is the right of the people to alter or to abolish it."

God treats everyone with justice, impartiality, and love. If agents violate these "self-evident truths," they become disqualified. Thus, a concept of individual rights is inherently a part of the morality of the Western mode of organization. People should respect each other's rights. Organizations also should protect individual rights. To prevent the misuse of power by agents in organizations, constitutions have come into being. The concept of constitutions is coordinated with the Western concept of public service. The state may ask for people's service, but it must promise not to infringe on their rights. The state should exercise power only within the scope of justice.

I have talked a lot about the morality inherent in Western organizational patterns. My purpose has been to provide a contrast to the characteristics of morality found in the Chinese mode of association. In these self-centered networks of social relationships, the most important feature is certainly *ke ji fu li* (subdue the self and follow the rites). "From the Son of Heaven down to ordinary people, all must consider the cultivation of the person as the root of everything.¹ This idea is the starting point in the system of morality inherent in Chinese social structure.

Extending out from the self are the social spheres formed by one's personal relationships. Each sphere is sustained by a specific type of social ethic. The process by which the social spheres extend outward takes various paths, but the basic path is through kinship, which includes relations between parents and children and among siblings born of the same parents. The ethical values that match this sphere are filial piety and fraternal duty. "Filial piety and fraternal submission—are they not the foundation of a moral life?"² An additional route out from the self is through friends. The ethical values that match friendship are loyalty (*zhong*) and sincerity (*xin*). As Confucius said, "When acting on another's behalf, shouldn't you always be loyal? When dealing with friends, shouldn't you always be sincere? . . . Make loyalty and sincerity your first principles. Have no friends who do not measure up to yourself."³ Confucius once concluded, "A young man, when at home, should be filial, and when out in the world should be respectful to his elders. He should be earnest and truthful. He should overflow with love, and cultivate the friendship of the good."⁴

Now I must mention a more complicated concept, *ren* (benevolence). As I have said, the Chinese pattern of social organization embraces no ethical concepts that transcend specific types of human relationships, as is the case in the West. Filial piety, fraternal duty, loyalty, and sincerity—these are all ethical principles found in private personal relationships. Confucius, however, frequently mentioned *ren*. In the *Analects*, he explained *ren* more than any other concept, but these explanations were also the most elusive. On the one hand, he repeatedly tried to clarify the meaning of the word; on the other hand, "In his conversations, Confucius seldom spoke of profit, destiny, and benevolence."⁵ On several occasions,

---

1. *The Great Learning*, sec. 6.   2. *Analects*, Book 1, chap. 2.
3. Ibid., Book 1, chaps. 3 and 8.   4. Ibid., Book 1, chap. 6.
5. Ibid., Book 9, chap. 1. Fei here is pointing out a contradiction in the *Analects*. There are frequent references to *ren*, but no precise definition, despite attempts by Confucius's disciples to obtain one.

Confucius was simply unable to express what he seemed to have on his mind.

"Sima Niu asked Confucius about *ren*. The Master said, 'A man possessing *ren* is cautious and slow in speaking.' Niu asked, 'Is this what is meant by *ren*?' The Master said, 'Acting in a benevolent way is difficult. Is it any wonder that one should be reluctant to speak?' "[6] At another point, Confucius said, "I have never met a person who loves *ren*. There may be such a case, but I have never seen it."[7] At yet another point, when Meng Wubo asked whether Zilu was *ren*, Confucius said, "I cannot say." When Meng Wubo repeated the question, the Master said, "In a government of a state of even a thousand chariots, a man can be given the responsibility of managing the army, but whether he is *ren* or not I cannot say." He was asked, "What about Qiu?" Confucius replied, "Qiu can be given the responsibility of being the steward in a town with a thousand households or in a noble family with a hundred chariots, but whether he is *ren* or not I cannot say." "What about Chi?" Confucius said, "When Chi puts on his finery and takes his place at court, he can be given the responsibility of conversing with the honored guests, but whether he is *ren* or not I cannot say."[8]

Many times, Confucius observed that what someone did "is insufficient to prove benevolence." But when he tried to explain *ren* in a positive way, he always returned to the ethical qualities in personal relationships: "Subduing yourself and submitting to ritual is what constitutes *ren*." He also said, "Whoever is able to put five things into practice throughout the whole world is certainly *ren*. These are earnestness, consideration for others, trustworthiness, diligence, and generosity. If you are earnest, you will never meet with disrespect. If you are considerate to others, you will win the people's hearts. If you are trustworthy, people will trust you. If you are diligent, you will be successful in your undertakings. If you are generous, you will find plenty of people who are willing to serve you."[9]

Confucius's difficulty is that, with a loosely organized rural society such as China's, it was not easy to find an all-encompassing ethical concept. The concept of *ren* is, in fact, only a logical synthe-

---

6. Ibid., Book 12, chap. 3.   7. Ibid., Book 4, chap. 6.
8. Ibid., Book 5, chap. 7.   9. Ibid., Book 7, chap. 6.

sis, a compilation of all the ethical qualities of private, personal relationships. Chinese social patterns, unlike Western ones, lack organizations that transcend individual personal relationships. In China, there was only the all-encompassing *tianxia* (everything under heaven), as in the phrase "Everything under heaven returns to *ren*." *Tianxia* matches *ren* in its ambiguity, and so *ren* cannot be more clearly defined than *tianxia*. Therefore, whenever Confucius wanted to clarify *ren*, he had to return to the ethical principles of individual relationships: filial piety, fraternal duty, loyalty, and sincerity. Similarly, when he tried to clarify *tianxia*, he had to return to concrete relationships themselves, such as those between fathers and sons, between older and younger brothers, and among friends.

In the traditional Chinese system of morality, there is no concept of "love" such as that which exists in Christianity—universal love without distinctions. It is even hard to find ethical principles linking individuals with groups. In the organizational patterns in Western society, public service, in the sense of fulfilling obligations toward a group, is a clearly defined social norm. In Chinese traditional society, however, there is no such norm. Nowadays we sometimes use the word *zhong* (loyalty) to convey this meaning, but the meaning of the word *zhong* as given in the *Analects* is quite different. In the sentence "When acting on another's behalf, shouldn't you always be loyal?" the word *loyal* really means "to be sincere with others"; it is another way of indicating inner emotions, of saying something is heartfelt.

In the *Analects*, Zizhang asked Confucius his opinion of the minister Ziwen: "In his public life he was made prime minister three times, and yet on none of these occasions did he show any sign of elation. Three times he was dismissed from office, and on none of these occasions did he show any sign of resentment. He was always careful, when giving up office, to explain to his successor the line of policy which the government had been pursuing under his administration. Now, what do you think of him?" Confucius answered, "He was *zhong* (loyal)."[10] In this passage, *zhong* means something close to loyalty to one's duty, but it does not mean loyalty to an organization. As a matter of fact, in the *Analects*, *zhong* is

10. Ibid., Book 5, chap. 18.

not even a principle of the relationship between a ruler and his officials. There, the principle linking ruler and official is *yi* (righteousness, correctness). As Confucius said, "A gentleman who takes office tries to carry out what he thinks to be right."[11] The concept of the "loyal official" came later. Furthermore, loyalty to the ruler is itself not an ethical principle joining the individual to an organization but, rather, signifies a personal relationship between ruler and officials.

This absence of an organizational morality can be seen even more clearly in the conflict between the public and the private spheres. Though responsible for governing the empire, the emperor still had first to fulfill the obligations of his personal relationships. According to Mencius,

> Tao Ying asked, "When Shun was emperor and Gaoyao was the judge, if Shun's father had killed a man, what should have happened?"
> Mencius said, "Gaoyao would have arrested him."
> "In that case, would Shun not have tried to stop it?"
> "How could Shun have stopped it? Gaoyao would have had the authority to deal with the matter."
> "Then what would Shun have done?"
> "Shun would have regarded abandoning the empire as throwing away a worn-out shoe. He would have secretly carried the old man on his back and fled to the edge of the sea. He would have lived there all his life happily and forgotten all about the empire."[12]

All this is to say that, although Shun was the emperor, he was still unable to treat his father as he would any other subject. Mencius's answer is an ideal solution to the conflict between the public and the private. Shun tried to serve two goals, but could not. Mencius thought of a way to escape the law by Shun's living in a remote place by the sea.

Mencius was able to give this answer because this example was fictitious. However, in another place, Mencius dealt with a problem in a way that demonstrates even more clearly the absence of universalism in Chinese moral standards.

11. Ibid., Book 18, chap. 7.
12. *The Works of Mencius*, Book 7, chap. 35. *The Works of Mencius*, included among the four great books of Confucian learning, is a compilation of writings and dialogues attributed to Mencius.

Wan Zhang said, "Xiang was daily engaged in plotting against Shun's life. When Shun became the emperor, why did he only banish his brother?"

Mencius said, "He enfeoffed him; some only called it banishment."

Wan Zhang said, "Shun banished Gonggong to Youzhou, Huandou to Mount Chong, Sanmiao to Sanwei, and Gun to Mount Yu, where he died. When these four culprits were punished, the people in the Empire bowed to the will of Shun, because it was the punishment of the wicked. Xiang was the most wicked of them all; yet he was enfeoffed in Youbi. What wrong had the people of Youbi done? Is that the way a benevolent man behaves? Others he punished, but when it came to his own brother, he enfeoffed him."

Mencius replied, "A benevolent man neither harbors anger nor nurses resentment against a brother. All he does is to love him. Because he loves him, he wishes him to have rank. Because he loves him, he wishes him to be rich. To enfeoff him in Youbi was to enrich him and let him have rank. If as emperor he had allowed his brother to remain a common man, could that be described as loving him?"[13]

A society with a differential mode of association is composed of webs woven out of countless personal relationships. To each knot in these webs is attached a specific ethical principle. For this reason, the traditional moral system was incapable of producing a comprehensive moral concept. Therefore, all the standards of value in this system were incapable of transcending the differential personal relationships of the Chinese social structure.

The degree to which Chinese ethics and laws expand and contract depend on a particular context and how one fits into that context. I have heard quite a few friends denounce corruption, but when their own fathers stole from the public, they not only did not denounce them but even covered up the theft. Moreover, some went so far as to ask their fathers for some of the money made off the graft, even while denouncing corruption in others. When they themselves become corrupt, they can still find comfort in their "capabilities." In a society characterized by a differential mode of association, this kind of thinking is not contradictory. In such a society, general standards have no utility. The first thing to do is to understand the specific context: Who is the important figure, and what kind of relationship is appropriate with that figure?

13. Ibid., Book 5, Part I, chap. 3.

Only then can one decide the ethical standards to be applied in that context.

In a society based on a Western organizational mode of association, people in the same organizations apply universal moral principles to themselves and so regard each other as equals. This kind of thinking, however, is exactly what Mencius most opposed. He said, "That things are unequal is part of their nature. . . . If you reduce them to the same level, it will only bring confusion to the empire."[14] Motzu's idea about universal love is exactly opposite to the Confucian idea of differential human relationships. It is for this reason that Mencius accused Motzu of being both fatherless and rulerless.[15]

14. Ibid., Book 3, chap. 4.
15. Motzu was the founder of an important school of Chinese philosophy that is roughly a contemporary of Confucianism and was one of the contending schools of thought during the Warring States period (480–221 B.C.). One of the principal ideas he emphasized was an all-embracing love.

6

Patrilineages

In the last two chapters, I discussed first the relations between groups and individuals and then patterns of social structure. I proposed several concepts—in particular, "differential mode of association" (*chaxugeju*) and "organizational mode of association" (*tuantigeju*). I knew that these unfamiliar terms would cause troubles for my readers, but I had to create them in order to conceptualize clearly those contexts that are currently absent from sociological terminology. I am not entirely satisfied with the terms I used, and I know they can lead to some misunderstandings. For instance, after reading my analysis in the last chapter, a friend of mine shook his head and said that he could not agree with my conclusion that there are no organizations in Chinese rural society. He pointed to families, lineages, neighborhoods, communities, and villages. What are they if not organizations? Obviously, we used the same term to define different things. In order to distinguish the distinctive patterns underlying the two kinds of social groups, I narrowed the conventional meaning for the term *organization*, applying it only to groups having a continuous organizational pattern. I used this term to accentuate the contrast with groups having a differential mode of association. Those groups I called "social circles" (*shehui quanzi*) instead of the more common term *organizations*. All social groups are organized in some fashion. Most of those groups mentioned by my friend conform in nature to what I have defined as "social circles." But let me clarify this some more. I do not mean to say that there are no "organizations" in Chinese rural society or that all groups have the characteristics of a social circle. For example, rotating credit associations (*qianhui*) obviously have an organizational pattern.[1] In my analysis, I wanted to discuss only the pre-

1. *Qianhui* (rotating credit associations) are a set group of people, each of whom contributes a specified sum of money that is then loaned to members of the

dominant pattern; in Chinese rural society, the pattern formed by differential relationships and social circles is more important than other patterns. Similarly, differential relationships also exist in modern Western societies, but they are not as important there. The two types of patterns represent basic forms of social structure that can be distinguished in concept but often coexist in reality. Nonetheless, we can see that the different patterns gain predominance in different settings.

It is essential to differentiate conceptually between the two types of social groups and the two ways of organizing, because the distinction helps us even better to understand social structures and thereby to avoid confusion. In this chapter, I will continue to use this set of concepts to examine the nature of the most basic group in Chinese rural society, the family (*jia*).

The most common group in rural society is generally called the "large family" (*da jiating*). In *Peasant Life in China*, I called this group the "expanded family." The important part of these two terms is "family" (*jiating*). I added the adjectives "large" or "small" to "family" in order to show that, although Chinese and Western families are the same in nature, they are different in form. But now my viewpoint has changed. I think the terminology is no longer appropriate. Instead, a more appropriate term for identifying the most basic unit in Chinese rural society is "small lineage" (*xiao jiazu*).

I suggest this new term because I want to clarify the difference in the structural principles of Chinese and Western "families." The difference between the so-called big and small family is not one of size, not one concerning the number of people who can be included, but one of structure. A family with more than ten children does not constitute a "large family," while a family of four people—containing the husband, wife, their son, and their daughter-in-law—should not be called a "small family." The first is larger than the second in number, but the second is more complicated than the first in structure. The two families incorporate different principles.

In anthropology, there is a clear definition of the concept of fam-

---

group. Borrowers repay the loan with an agreed-upon interest. Even today, it is a common way of raising money without going to banks.

ily: A family is the procreative group formed by parents and their children. The parent-child relationship indicates the structure, and procreation is the function. This definition suggests a bilateral kinship system, which simultaneously stresses both the father's side and the mother's side of the family. The sons and daughters are the children produced by the couple. The purpose of such a social union is to give birth and raise children. In societies where each individual must bear the task of raising children, there will be many of these procreative groups. But for each of these families, the function of procreation is fulfilled in a relatively short time span. The children quickly grow up and leave their parents' care, and then they, too, take on the tasks of giving birth to and raising their own children. This process continues generation after generation. For this reason, it is in the nature of the family group to be temporary. In this respect, the group composed of a family is not the same as other common types of social groups. Groups such as schools and states are not considered temporary, although in reality they certainly do not continue forever. They are not temporary, because both fulfill functions that last over the long term. But insofar as the family is considered to have only procreation as its function, the family might as well prepare to end shortly after it begins. The purpose of having children ends when they are raised. I have discussed this issue in detail in the book *Systems of Reproduction*.[2]

In every culture, however, the family always has other functions besides procreation. The cooperation of a husband and wife does not end when their children grow up. There are periods, at the beginning of the union as well as after the children have grown, when a couple will be by themselves. Between the two, there will be economic, emotional, and sexual cooperation, but what the two of them can accomplish just by themselves will be very limited. To accomplish most things requires the joint effort of a lot of people; therefore, these things must be managed by other kinds of social groups.

In the West, families are groups that have an organizational character. As I explained earlier, Western families have strict boundaries. For this reason, they are able to manage few things beyond raising children. But in Chinese rural society, families do

2. Fei Xiaotong, *Shengyu zhidu* (Shanghai: Shangwu, 1947).

not have strict organizational boundaries. These groups can expand, as needed, by incorporating ever more distant categories of
relatives. Those people who make up the family and who form
what I have called social circles are not limited to parents and children. Nonetheless, the manner of expansion is limited by social
structure. For Chinese families, the route of expansion is patrilineal; it incorporates only those from the father's side of the family.
With few exceptions, families do not include daughters-in-law and
sons-in-law at the same time.[3] According to the patrilineal principle, married daughters and their husbands, the sons-in-law, are
outside the family. But on the paternal side, the family can be expanded to include very distant kin. A family with five generations
under the same roof would include all paternal relatives in all five
generations.

Anthropologists call the social group organized on the patrilineal or matrilineal kinship principle a "lineage." Structurally,
Chinese families are lineages. Lineage (*shizu*) is not exactly the same
as what we commonly refer to as the clan (*zu*). What we call a clan
is really a number of lineages whose members have the same sur-
name.[4] Therefore, I will use the term *small lineage* to indicate a sin-
gle-lineage social group. Small and large lineages rest on the same
structural principles, but they differ in number and in size. That is
why I prefer not to use the term *large family* to identify a lineage.
By using the term *small lineage*, I emphasize the structural characteristics of the Chinese family and not just the size.

The lineage structure includes the household. The smallest lineage may, in fact, be equal to a nuclear family household. Kinship
structure is based on the relationship between parents and children, which is the triangle formed by the father, mother, and child.
A lineage expands out from this household family base. But in a
lineage the nuclear family is only one ring in a structure of concentric social circles. We cannot say that the nuclear family household
does not exist, but we should never think of it as an independent
unit, as an organization unto itself.

Differences in social structure produce variations in behavior.

3. Married daughters usually live with their husbands' families. When a family
does not have a son, the parents may want their daughter to marry a man who is
willing to move in with them.

4. For a discussion of the distinction between lineage and clan, see Hugh Baker,
Chinese Family and Kinship (New York: Columbia University Press, 1979).

Although one of the functions of a lineage is to raise and educate children, it is not limited to that function. From an anthropological perspective, a lineage is a way of organizing activity; when a single lineage joins other lineages in a common frame of action, the group becomes what anthropologists call a "tribe." Lineages and tribes have complex political, economic, and religious functions. This is true for Chinese families as well. It is my hypothesis that Chinese rural society took on a differential mode of association when kinship was successfully used as a medium to create social groups and to manage all kinds of activities. Not until that time did the Chinese family change into a lineage-based structure. This fact is important on two counts. First, in Chinese rural society, lineages carry the responsibility for political, economic, religious, and other functions. Second, in order to handle so much activity, the family structure cannot be limited to simple combinations of parents and children but must expand outward. Moreover, because politics, economy, religion, and social activity all require long-term continuity, the basic social groups certainly cannot be as transitory as Western families. The family must have continuity. It must not break up when the children grow up and must not end when individual members die. Therefore, the family has incorporated the qualities of a lineage, becoming a lineage unto itself. A lineage is long-term, and so are our families. I call this kind of social group a "small lineage," to emphasize its inherent long-term qualities. The Chinese family is the opposite of a temporary household.

The Chinese family is a medium through which all activities are organized. The size of the family depends on the extent of the activity being organized. If an activity is small enough for husband and wife to handle, the family can be as small as a single household; but if the enterprise goes beyond what the couple can manage, then brothers and uncles may all join in to form what now becomes a large family. In Chinese rural society, therefore, the size of families varies a great deal. But no matter how much the size may vary, the structural principle, the patrilineal pattern of differential relationships, always remains the same.

In any society, when the group whose principal task is procreation begins to take on many other functions, changes necessarily occur in the relationships between the members of that group. In the organization of Western families, husband and wife are the main axis, and together they manage the task of raising children. Playing a supporting role, the children leave this organization when they become adults. In the West, political, economic, and religious functions are the responsibility of other organizations and are not included among the tasks of households. Husband and wife are central players around whom everything else moves, and the force that holds them together as a couple is their emotional attachment. The emotional quality of this union has made the family serve as the main source of solace and comfort in Western life. In my book *The American Character*, I describe the family as a "life fortress."[5]

In Chinese rural society, however, there are obvious differences in the nature of the family. Our families have long-term continuity and serve as means to organize other activities. The main axes of the family are between father and son and between mother and daughter-in-law. These are vertical, not horizontal, relationships. The husband-wife relationship plays a minor role. Nonetheless, the relations between husband and wife, as well as the relations along the main axes of the family, are never temporary. But these family attachments have been stripped of "ordinary emotions" by the demands of a family's practical activities. What I call "ordinary emotions" stand in contrast to discipline. No enterprise can abandon considerations of efficiency. In order to obtain efficiency, one must have strict discipline. But discipline does not tolerate personal feelings. All Chinese families have family rules. Between husband and wife, there should be mutual respect. For women, there are "the three followings and the four virtues."[6] Between father and son, there should be responsibility for the father and obedience for the son. These are the special characteristics of groups designed for enterprise.

In wealthy families and in families devoted to scholarship, men and women often live in separate parts of the household, women being consigned to the inner quarters and men living in the outer portions of the house. But this separation is also psychological, and

5. Fei Xiaotong, *Meiguoren xingge* (Shanghai: Shenghuo, 1947).
6. "The three followings and the four virtues" are precepts that come from the book *Nüjie* (Lessons for women) by Banzhao, a female scholar of the Han period. The three followings mean that a woman's status follows that of her father before marriage, her husband during marriage, and her son in widowhood. The four virtues the women should cultivate are (1) women's moral virtues, (2) women's speech, (3) women's appearance, and (4) women's work.

even extends to rural villages, where it is common to see an obvious indifference between husbands and wives. When I conducted surveys in rural areas, I paid special attention to this problem. Later, during the war, when I was evacuated to the countryside, I lived with a farm family for a long time and was even more struck by this fact. Most rural couples I know say that they have "little use for words" or that they "really have nothing to talk about" with each other. From the time people get up in the morning, they are so fully occupied with their work that they have no time to chat. If the women do not work in the fields, they stay at home taking care of children. After a day's work, men usually do not stay at home. In fact, a man is regarded as spineless if he likes to hang around with his wife. So a man goes out whether he has business to attend to or not. Teahouses, tobacco stores, even street corners and alleyways—these are the places where men go to idle away their time and to find emotional comfort. There they talk, laugh, and have a really good time. When they return home, the husband and wife cooperate smoothly, each doing what is expected of him or her. As long as everything goes smoothly, there is nothing special to talk about, and so there is no need to talk. If things are not going well, they may start to quarrel or even have a fight. You cannot call this intimacy. These observations made me feel that the emotional life of Western and of rural Chinese families cannot be discussed in the same terms. In rural areas, talking, laughing, and showing emotion and affection openly occur only in groups composed of people of the same sex and age. Men get together only with other men, women with other women, and children with other children. Except for matters of work and reproduction, people of different sexes and ages maintain considerable distance.

This separation by age and sex is certainly not accidental. In my opinion, it results from the family's taking on many functions other than just procreation. The emotional life of the Chinese is not the same as that of Westerners. Emotion among the Chinese, especially between the sexes, is characterized by reserve and restraint, and cannot be displayed openly as it can in the West. It is this social environment, an environment dominated by lineages, that nurtures this Chinese personality.

7

"Between Men and Women, There Are Only Differences"

In the previous chapter, I said that Chinese rural society is composed of groups devoted to activities, to enterprises. Wherever they exist, such groups must maintain discipline, and discipline necessarily excludes personal sentiments. With this point, we face the basic question about the orientation of emotions within the Chinese tradition. I discussed this question briefly in the last chapter. In this chapter, I will elaborate further.

By using the term *emotional orientation*, I want to point out that people develop a direction or orientation to their feelings. This direction is shaped by cultural norms. Therefore, when we analyze these cultural patterns, we should pay attention to the directions in which cultural norms allow personal emotions to develop. We will call this cultural shaping of emotions the "emotional orientation."

Emotions can be analyzed from two perspectives. Psychology explains the nature and kinds of emotions by observing physiological changes in the body. Sociology, however, will look at the role of emotions as they occur within social relationships. Happiness, anger, sorrow, and joy are certainly physiological phenomena, but they always happen in the context of human life and always have an influence on human relationships. It is only as social phenomena that emotions, like other human actions, obtain their significance.

Psychology defines emotions as internal behavior that manifests itself in external ways. William James said that emotion is a change in one's internal disposition.[1] This change forms a tendency to act, a sort of bodily tension, a force capable of launching behavior. If

1. The reference is to William James, *Principles of Psychology* (New York: Henry Holt, 1890).

the connection between a certain stimulus and a given response is customary, the response will be stable and automatic; no inner tension, and hence no strong emotions, will be produced. Emotion always occurs when an old response is blocked and a new response is attempted. When this happens, what we mean by emotions is much the same as what we mean when we say that we are "getting excited" or that we are "fired up." In fact, using "fire" as a metaphor for emotions indicates this state of readiness, of being tense. In social relationships, such emotion can be used either for destructive or for creative purposes. The immediacy and excitement of emotions change the original relationships. In other words, if one wants to maintain stable social relationships, one needs to avoid situations that cause emotional agitation. In fact, indifference is an indication of stable social relationships. This is the reason I said in the previous chapter that discipline excludes personal feelings.

The force that stabilizes social relationships is not emotion (*ganqing*) but understanding (*liaojie*). Understanding means accepting a common frame of reference. The same stimulus will call forth the same response. In the two chapters on literacy in the countryside, I mentioned that propinquity and familiarity breed a mutual awareness. Such feelings of mutuality and a condition of being emotional are completely at odds with each other. Mutuality rests on a harmony that is continuously reproduced. Mutuality is silent, whereas emotionality needs to be voiced. Singing, crying, shouting—these are all indispensable accompaniments to emotional excitement.

In *The Decline of the West*, Oswald Spengler writes that two cultural patterns characterize Western civilization.[2] He calls one pattern "Apollonian" and the other "Faustian." Apollonian patterns rest on a belief that the universe consists of a perfect order that is beyond the creative power of human beings to alter. Human beings can only accept this order, be content with it, and maintain it. But if human beings do not have the capacity to maintain the world as it is, the paradise will be lost and the golden age will pass away. This is the spirit of classical antiquity. Modern culture, according

2. Oswald Spengler, *The Decline of the West*, trans. Charles F. Atkinson (New York: Knopf, 1926).

to Spengler, is Faustian. Conflicts are the basis of existence. To live is to overcome obstacles; without obstacles, life loses its significance. All that human beings can see in the future is the process of endless creation and continuous changes.

These two cultural perspectives can be used to understand the differences in emotional orientation between rural and modern societies. Rural society is Apollonian; modern society is Faustian. The difference in the spirit manifest in the two types of cultures also shows up in the most basic patterns of social life in the two types of societies.

Rural society depends on intimate and long-term cooperation to coordinate the interactions of individuals. Their social contacts are so well developed and so familiar that rural people do things automatically to a certain extent. Only living and dying in the same place, generation after generation, will create such intimate groups. In such a place, people develop a high degree of mutual understanding. They have similar likes and dislikes, and even smell the same. To reach such a state requires one precondition, that there should be no major difference among people to impede their mutual understanding. Spatial location is not a factor preventing rural people from understanding each other. Being isolated and having only few contacts with other groups, rural people live in a small world. Each generation lives the same life cycle as the previous generation—birth, aging, sickness, then death—and each experiences these in much the same way. The young have not experienced the life of a person who has passed into old age, so they do not understand an older person's frame of mind. For this reason, age differences contribute to a lack of mutual understanding. This lack of understanding occurs only on the part of the young, because older people can understand the young and even predict the problems they will face. But when the young look upon the old as a reference point for their own lives, what we might regard as a lack of understanding does not at the same time result in a generation gap.

In rural society, it is the differences in biology that prevent people who live closely together from obtaining a full understanding of each other. These biological differences are certainly not characteristics transmitted by heredity, for such hereditary differences are not so obvious in small communities where families intermarry generation after generation. The biological differences that eternally divide people are the sexual differences between men and women. No one has ever personally experienced what it is to be a member of the opposite sex, so our exact knowledge of that difference can only be indirect and superficial. In reality, everyone has, at some point, felt a lack of mutual understanding between the sexes. We have no way to comprehend the content of that difference; we can only guess.

Even in a society where people base their behavior on mutual familiarity, the sexual divide remains a fundamental obstacle. Only in heaven is this split between the sexes overcome. It is no accident that many religions, whether consciously or unconsciously, deny the fact of gender. Perfect morality and absolute justice must be based on complete understanding, a condition that presumes no obstacles. They cannot be sought (or found) in a society that has as one of its foundations the gap between men and women.

The biological differences between men and women are for the sake of reproducing the species. The union of men and women is guided by this fact. It is a union based on differences, not on similarities. To seek a perfect understanding on the basis of these differences is difficult. That path is full of obstacles, because it requires people to search creatively for some greater unity between the sexes. This is a Faustian attempt. Faust is the symbol of emotion. He regarded ever-changing, ever-surging emotions as his lifeblood. The Faustian effort is an unending one, because a final unity can never be achieved. The Faustian effort is only a process that searches for unity. Moreover, the more that men and women attempt to create a common life, the deeper the degree of their differences and the larger the obstacles to unity become. This growing struggle requires yet stronger creative powers to overcome the obstacles. In the Faustian view, life's force becomes stronger and life's meaning more profound because of the unending struggle.

A Faustian style of love between the sexes is inappropriate for a relationship culminating in reproduction. Faustian love is an adventure, an exploration into the unknown. It differs from friendship, in that friendship may stop at a certain level of understanding. Faustian love, however, never stops; it only pursues. The effort that goes into this kind of love does not have practical purposes—

either for economic production or for any enterprising activity. Rather, it is an effort to create one's own life experiences, an effort to create the meaning of life itself. If this kind of love is to persist, one must constantly re-create the love relationship by continuously discovering and overcoming obstacles. What one wants to achieve is the process itself, not the results of the process. In fact, those results may be of no importance whatsoever. This struggle to achieve an unending love makes social relationships unstable. Moreover, activities that rely on such social relationships cannot be easily managed. If we look at modern culture, we see that the changes occurring in the emotional relationships between men and women have already disrupted the process of creating families. Unless we find other ways for society to operate, the Faustian spirit will destroy our society's most fundamental activity—its own patterns of procreation.

Rural society does not allow the Faustian spirit. Rural society does not need to create new social relationships. Social relationships are fixed from the time of birth. Rural society seeks stability, so it fears the destruction of social relationships. It is Apollonian. The relationship between men and women must be arranged so that their emotional states are not erratic. That is what the principle "Between men and women, there are only differences" actually means.[3] One need not seek an underlying commonality between men and women; between them, there should be some distance. This distancing is clearly present in the prescription "There should be no intimacy in the interaction between men and women."[4] This distancing is not just physical but also psychological. Although they act in concert, men and women should manage their respective economic and reproductive activities by strictly following assigned rules of behavior. They should not hope to achieve mental or emotional harmony with each other.

As I mentioned in the last chapter, Chinese social structure promotes many associations that join people of the same sex together. The presence of such associations can be clearly seen in Chinese rural society. The principles underlying such same-sex associations

3. This phrase originally comes from the *Liji* (Book of rites). The *Liji* is regarded as one of the Confucian classics. It was compiled during the Western Han period (206 B.C.–A.D. 8) and contains early discussion of ritual practices.
4. *The Works of Mencius*, Book 4, chap. 17.

and the formation of nuclear families would seem to be at odds, because the family's function of procreation is based on a hetero-sexual union. Accordingly, the cohesion of individual households in rural society would seem to be affected by—indeed, to be threat-ened by—the presence of all those same-sex associations. In rural society, however, lineages serve as a substitute for individual fam-ilies, and lineages give priority to alliances among people of the same sex. In lineages, heterosexual relationships complement but do not necessarily contradict the dominant pattern. In Chinese ru-ral society, lineages are the basic social unit and are an expression of the relative importance of the principle underlying same-sex as-sociations.

The same principle underlies the dictum "Between men and women, there are only differences." People's understanding of this principle has caused them to develop emotional attachments to people of the same sex. We cannot say for sure how common ho-mosexuality and narcissism are. But many sworn brother- and sisterhoods in rural society seek a level of intimacy that is conveyed in the saying "Friends wish not to be born but, rather, to die on the same day." Thus, the emotional orientation toward having close relationships among people of the same sex is already quite pro-found. Extreme examples of this pattern, involving women, are the sisterhood associations in South China and, in literature, the Feng Xiaoqing genre of women's writing, which takes on a narcissistic tone.[5] It is a shame that we have not analyzed the emotional life of Chinese people very much. Because so little has been done, my discussion on this topic has to stop here.

Because men and women do not spend time chasing after some-one of the opposite sex in search of unending love, there is in this society one less source of impractical diversions. The pragmatic spirit of Chinese rural society embraces a quality of "this-worldli-ness." Confucians do not talk about ghosts. Confucius himself said that one should "sacrifice to the spirits as if the spirits were pres-

---

5. Feng Xiaoqing is believed to have lived in the Yangzhou area during the Ming dynasty (1368–1644). She was talented in writing poetry and painting. When she was sixteen years old, her parents sent her to the Feng family in Hangzhou as a concubine. Feng's wife was very jealous of her and forced her to move into a nun-nery. There she supposedly died of a broken heart at the age of eighteen. In later years, her life story was used as the basis for stories and plays. At the nunnery, she is said to have written many poems full of self-pity, and hence the narcissistic tone.

ent."[6] Apparently, even teachers of religion had no real interest in anything beyond this life. Ordinary people go even further; they secularize heaven itself. They do not want to use a utopian vision to change reality and to realize a heaven on earth. Instead, they regard the present reality as a working draft of what heaven must be like and therefore push this world into heaven itself. People see living as a matter of restraining oneself in order to accommodate to an outside world. In other words, one must change oneself internally so that one can fit externally into an established order. That is the reason we can say that Chinese rural society conforms to the patterns of antiquity—that it is Apollonian.

The social order restrains and contains individuality. In order to protect itself, it suppresses all potentially destructive forces. The distance between men and women is built on this suppression. Rural society is a society in which "between men and women, there are only differences." For this reason, it is also a stable society.

6. *Analects*, Book 3, chap. 12.

8

A Rule of Ritual

It is conventional to contrast "a rule of people" to "a rule of law" and to categorize Western societies as ruled by laws and our society as ruled by people. Actually, this contrast is not very accurate. A rule of law does not mean that the law itself rules and maintains social order but, rather, that human relationships in the society are sustained according to laws. Laws depend on political power for their support and on people for their execution. Therefore, rule by law actually means both that *people use laws to rule* and, of course, that human factors are involved.

Some modern legal theorists place great weight on the human factors that influence laws.[1] They emphasize that, when a law is applied in a specific case, a judge must render an interpretation based on a legal statute. Although the object of the judge's interpretation may be that legal text, what is included in a specific judgment results from many factors. The judge's biases, whether he has a stomachache or not, the state of public opinion—all these and other factors may be very important. Therefore, these legal theorists think that the law is nothing but a judge's judgment. This itself is a one-sided view. Judges cannot render a decision just as they please. At a minimum, the decision must be seen to be based in law. Nonetheless, this view should remind us that human factors are always involved in a rule of law.

What, then, is the distinction between a rule of people and a rule of law? If ruling by people is the opposite of ruling by laws, does that mean that *people do not use laws to rule?* If ruling means the maintenance of social order, one can hardly imagine a social order that could be maintained without any force whatsoever. It is

---

1. Fei is referring here to the theorists from the school of legal realism, which was then important in the United States. For a brief summary of this school, see Grant Gilmore, *The Ages of American Law* (New Haven, Conn.: Yale University Press, 1977).

equally difficult to imagine that human interaction could be coordinated automatically without any rules or norms. If a society is not run according to laws, how is it run? If we take the words literally, a rule of people would seem to mean that powerful people can, at their whim, establish the social rules for human relationships. I doubt very much that this kind of "rule by the people" could ever happen. If people who live together had no norms to guide their interaction and no regulations to fix their rights and responsibilities, and if they did everything only according to the ruler's unpredictable whims, the society would be in absolute chaos. People would not know how to act. That situation could not happen, and, in any event, it could not be called a system of rule, by whatever name.

The difference between ruling by people and ruling by laws does not lie in the words *people* and *law* but, rather, in the force used to maintain order and in the nature of the social norms.

Maintaining a rural social order differs, in many respects, from maintaining a modern social order. But that does not mean that rural society is "without laws and without heaven" or that it "does not need laws," although that is the opinion of some people. Believing in a simple, natural life, Laotse thought that as long as a nation is simply a small community with few people—where one can hear the neighbors' chickens and dogs but never has to deal with the neighbors themselves—social order can be maintained without an exterior force. People will depend on their instincts and good sense, and the society will be peaceful. Laotse was not the only one to have this idea. The entire world economy has become intertwined and interrelated through modern systems of transportation; yet most people in the United States still believe in the theory of free competition as laid out in classical economics. Those Americans are opposed to humans' creating plans and regulations to maintain economic order; when there is free competition, they believe, an invisible hand automatically arranges for everyone a moral economic order. In various social, political, and economic professions, there are also those who regard anarchy as the ideal state. Certainly, anarchy does not equal chaos but, rather, is a type of order, a type that does not need laws. Hence, anarchy represents a kind of self-generated order, a society that is "ruled without being ruled."

But rural society is not of this kind either. We can say that it is a society "without law," if we define laws as those regulations maintained by state power. However, the absence of laws does not affect social order, because rural society is ruled by rituals.[2]

Let me clarify one point from the outset. The fact that a society is ruled through an etiquette established by rituals does not mean that the people in that society are gentle and refined. It is not like that country of highly civilized gentlemen depicted in the novel *Jing hua yuan*.[3] "Ritual etiquette" here does not convey the notion of manners—of being "cultured' or "benevolent" or even of "nodding to people you meet" and of not being atrocious. With ritual etiquette, one can kill others; one can be utterly barbaric. For instance, in India, there are some places where wives are expected to immolate themselves on their husbands' funeral pyres. This is ritual etiquette. In Burma, there are some places where boys, as their rite of passage into adulthood, must chop off several human heads; otherwise, they cannot establish themselves as men. In our own ancient novels, we often read about military rituals of offering people as a sacrifice to the flag. According to modern standards, such rituals may seem very cruel. But whether something is cruel or not is unrelated to whether something is a ritual or not. It is written in the *Analects*, "Zigong did not want his lamb slaughtered for a ceremony. But Confucius said, 'You love the lamb; I love the rites.' "[4] A sense of pity did not make Confucius agree to call off the ruthless deed.

Rituals are publicly recognized behavioral norms. If one behaves according to the rituals, then one's behavior is correct and proper. In this respect, rituals are the same as laws, because laws are also behavioral norms. The difference between a ritual and a law is the force used to maintain the norms. Laws are enforced through state power. The term *state* here means political power. Before modern states developed, tribes also held political power. But rituals do not

2. The Chinese term *li* has numerous meanings, including rites, ritual, and etiquette. We use the word *ritual* to translate the term, but in English "ritual" has a pejorative meaning that it does not have in Chinese.
3. *Jing hua yuan* is a novel from the Qing dynasty (1644–1911) written by Li Juchen. A translation is available in English: *Flowers in the Mirror* (London: Arena Books, 1965).
4. *Analects*, Book 4, chap. 7.

require any concrete structure of political power in order to be effective. Instead, ritual norms are maintained by tradition.

Tradition is accumulated social experience. The purpose of behavioral norms is to coordinate behavior—that is, action taken in concert with others—so that people can fulfill their social responsibilities. Social responsibilities are simply those necessities of life that each person in society must satisfy. People need to cooperate with each other and to adopt efficient techniques in order to obtain resources from the environment. These techniques cannot be designed anew by each individual person or even by small temporary groups. People have the ability to learn. Therefore, those results that work successfully for one generation can be taught to the next generation. This kind of accumulation over many generations produces a set of methods that help people in their lives. Therefore, when people are born, they are born into a world in which other people have already worked out ways to cope with the problems that they will likely encounter themselves. The newcomers only need to learn and practice the received wisdom from previous generations in order to be able to enjoy the pleasures of satisfying their own needs.

Culture itself is tradition. No society is without tradition. We do not have to be overly concerned about how to deal with the most basic things in life—food, clothes, shelter, and transportation—because, thanks to our ancestors, we have ready-made rules to follow. Tradition in rural society, however, is more important than it is in modern society, because it is more effective.

Rural society is a society of deep attachments, where people are born, live, and die in the same spot. Rural people move around very little, and the land from which they take their livelihood seldom changes. In this environment, people do not keep track of who is running the government. They live the same life generation after generation, trusting only their own experiences and those of their parents and grandparents. An old farmer standing in his fields encounters changes in seasons but not in eras. Every year, the same cycle is repeated. It is easy for people to borrow their ancestors' solutions to problems as a guide for their own lives. What proved effective in the previous generation is surely worth preserving. As the saying goes, "When one speaks, one has to mention Yao and

Shun'';[5] one has to know the past, because whatever security exists in life comes from following the old ways.

After the Japanese invasion of China, when my wife and I were evacuated to the countryside around Kunming, our newborn baby began to cry all the time. We could not find a doctor, so we had to ask our landlady for help. As soon as she heard the baby's cry, she knew that the baby had what she called ''a false tooth,'' a condition caused by a parasite. The ''tooth'' would hurt each time the baby breast-fed. But as soon as the baby stopped eating, she would cry because she was hungry. The landlady calmly told us to wipe the inside of the baby's mouth with pickles and blue cloth. After a day or two, the baby was well. It turned out that this was a local disease; every child got it, so every mother knew how to cure it. In this instance, experience was effective. As long as the environment does not change, as long as no new germs come in, this ''method without theory'' will always work. Because such methods work, there is no reason to seek the causes of their effectiveness.

In a tradition like that, you do not have to know why something works. Rather, you just have to follow the example of others. From knowing the past, one obtains those methods for ensuring one's own existence. Moreover, these methods are not isolated techniques; they are embedded in, and naturally carry with them, a set of values. When we say that some technique is ''effective'' (*ling-yan*), we mean that there is some unknown magic behind it. If you use that technique, you will have luck; if you don't, you will have problems. Therefore, people grow up in awe of tradition.

If we do not examine the relation between action and purpose, and if we only follow conventional methods in the belief that otherwise we will encounter misfortune, then the resulting sets of behavior will have a fixed ceremonial form. The meaning of ritual (*li*) is ''an act performed in accordance with ceremonial forms.'' The character *li* itself consists of two radicals, one signifying a tool used in rituals and the other signifying a type of ritual. Together, *li* means both the ritual itself and the action taken to conform to ritual.

A ritual (*li*) is not something that is carried out by an exterior force. Rituals work through the feeling of respect and of obedience

5. Yao and Shun are the legendary early rulers of China who established China's golden age.

that people themselves have cultivated. People conform to rituals on their own initiative. In fact, people can simply enjoy rituals. As the saying goes, "Being wealthy, one also loves the rituals" (*fu er hao li*). As is clear from the following conversation, even Confucius believed that people should act according to rituals on their own initiative:

> Yan Yuan asked about *ren*.
> The Master said, "To subdue oneself and conform to rituals is *ren*. If a man can for one day subdue himself and conform to rituals, all under heaven will ascribe *ren* to him. Is the practice of *ren* from a man himself, or is it from others?"
> Yan Yuan said, "I beg to ask the steps of that process."
> The Master replied, "Look not at what is contrary to rituals; listen not to what is contrary to rituals; speak not what is contrary to rituals."
> Yan Yuan then said, "Though I am deficient in intelligence and vigor, I will make it my business to practice this lesson."[6]

Ritual is obviously different from law and even from what we normally call morality. Law restrains people by setting external limits to action. The penalty for breaking a law is imposed on the individual by a designated power. People may break the law but escape being detected, and they may even feel proud of themselves or complacent if they succeed. Morality is sustained by public opinion. If you do something immoral or scandalous, people will ostracize you, and you will be shamed.

Ritual is even more exacting than morality. If you act in violation of rituals, your action is not only immoral but incorrect, and it will not bring about a desired result. Rituals are sustained by personal habits. It is as if there were ten eyes watching you and ten fingers pointing at you all the time. You cannot help but follow the ritual, even if you are all by yourself. Following rituals is the right way to act. Actually, it is a habit formed in the process of cultivating oneself. One learns to conform to tradition on one's own initiative.

On the surface, "a rule of rituals" seems like a self-generated form of social order in which people's actions are unrestrained by laws. Actually, "self-generated" is the wrong word here, because a rule of rituals implies that one uses one's own initiative to follow

---

6. *Analects*, Book 12, chap. 1.

conventional rules. Confucius often used the words *restrain* (*ke*) and *bind* (*yue*) to describe the process of ritual cultivation. These words suggest that "a rule of rituals" does not occur in the absence of society, does not stem from natural human instincts, and does not depend on directions from heaven.

A social order based on rituals has, as a precondition, a tradition that offers effective solutions to life's problems. Rural society meets this requirement. It is an order maintained by rituals. In societies that frequently change, the efficacy of tradition cannot be guaranteed. No matter how effective a solution was in the past, no one would follow the old ways to deal with new problems in a new environment. When a problem requires group cooperation, everyone in the group needs to agree on the methods used. And in order to ensure that everyone in the group uses the same methods at the same time to solve common problems, there needs to be some force to control each person. This is what a "rule of law" means.

A rule of laws and a rule of rituals occur in two different social circumstances. An order established through rituals may be the same as what some people commonly call "a rule of people." But "a rule of rituals" is a better term, because it will not be as easily misunderstood as the second term, which leads people to believe that a social order can be sustained by individual will. Ruling through rituals is very different from ruling through individuals. Rituals come from tradition, and the whole history of a society goes into maintaining this order. A society governed by rituals cannot easily appear in an era of rapid changes. But such a system of rule is characteristic of Chinese rural society.

9

A Society without Litigation

In rural society, if a person mentions the word *songshi*, a litigation monger, everyone thinks of a troublemaker, of someone who creates discord. Such people have no social status in this kind of society. In cities, however, not only do you have lawyers who promote litigation but you add the words "the honorable" to every lawyer's name, and what lawyers say and do is reported on the front page of every newspaper. Moreover, ordinary companies and individuals ask lawyers to serve as their permanent advisers. All this gives the impression to traditionally minded people that cities are full of disputes and are places where well-behaved people should not live.

Let us visualize now a change in emphasis in what a lawyer does. Instead of being a sort of legal shyster, a person who constantly quarrels over technicalities, the lawyer becomes a representative of a legal tradition. With this shift in emphasis, lawyers go from being instigators of disputes to being legal advisers. These two extremes nicely represent the changing nature of society itself. Instead of being governed through rituals, it now is governed through laws.

In urban societies, it is not shameful for a person who does not understand the law to ask others for advice. In fact, ordinary people living and working in cities are not likely to know all the various laws related to their lives and occupations. Law has become a specialized area of knowledge. Even so, people who have no knowledge of law cannot live outside of law, because to do so in an orderly urban society would disrupt people's sense of collective security. Therefore, many ordinary people have to have a lawyer to serve as their own legal adviser. Because of this requirement, lawyers have been able to elevate their social position.

However, in those rural societies where order is achieved through rituals, a person who does not know how to act according to rituals will be accused of behaving atrociously, of disregarding established norms, and of being morally bankrupt. To a county official in charge of the local order, the ideal means for maintaining an order based on ritual is through education, not through threatening to send people to prison. If a case has to end up in front of an official, then it is certain that someone has broken the traditional norms.

In the old novels from the imperial period, we often read about the process of hearing a case. It usually goes like this: The "convicts" are dragged to the main hall in the yamen. Each person, in turn, is beaten with a bamboo stick. Each party in the case then accuses the other party. Finally, the county official uses his insights into physiognomy to decide which person—by virtue of being uglier, slyer, or otherwise more repulsive—must be the perpetrator of the moral injustice. That person is then tortured until he or she confesses. Through confession, the good and bad will have been distinguished and set right. Justice having been administered, the people then will shout out their praises for the upright magistrate. From a modern point of view, this kind of process is irrational, but in rural society it is considered legitimate. Otherwise, why would stories based on this process, such as the cases of Magistrate Pao and Magistrate Shi, have become traditional best-sellers?[1]

In the last chapter, I explained how ruling through ritual is accomplished. Here I want to use an analogy to illustrate this idea further. In a soccer game, when the referee whistles and indicates that someone has committed a foul, that person has to accept the penalty. It is unnecessary for the two sides to stop the game and debate about the penalty. The ideal game is one in which the referee does nothing—except, of course, such things as starting the game and indicating when the ball goes out of bounds. Ideally, all the players are expected to know the rules of the game thoroughly before the game starts and to abide by those rules while they play the game. The referee is merely a person who is responsible for seeing that no player breaks the rules. It is not good sportsmanship

---

1. A few of these stories have been translated into English. See Leon Comber, *The Strange Cases of Magistrate Pao* (Hong Kong: Heinemann Educational Books, 1972), and Dee Goong An, *Three Murder Cases Solved by Judge Dee*, trans. Robert van Gulik (Tokyo: Toppan, 1949). Robert van Gulik has also written a number of Judge Dee mystery novels based on the Chinese originals.

for one player surreptitiously to hit another player behind the referee's back. If such incidents occur, and the player gets caught, the referee will penalize him, and his reputation as a player, and maybe even the reputation of the whole team, will suffer. Therefore, a player must be very familiar with the rules and must possess a level of skill that permits him to play spontaneously without breaking them. What he needs is a long period of training. If somebody deliberately commits a foul, that suggests he does not have adequate training, which in turn reflects badly on the coach.

This analogy may help explain rural society's view of litigation. A system of control based on rituals means adherence to traditional rules. All aspects of life and human relationships are governed by specific rules. All the actors in this society have been familiar with the rules since childhood, and they take those rules for granted. Their long education since childhood has turned these exterior rules into interior habits. The force to maintain rituals comes not from the outside but from the inside, from one's own conscience. Therefore, this social order pays a great deal of attention to self-cultivation and self-restraint. Ideally, in a society ruled through rituals, everyone will abide by the rules voluntarily, so that all exterior supervision is unnecessary. A person who surreptitiously breaks the rules for selfish reasons will be considered the scum of the earth. Understanding the rituals is everyone's responsibility. This society assumes that everyone will understand them, and it is this society's responsibility to make sure that everyone does understand them. Therefore, as we often say, "If the son is not taught, the fault lies with the father." In rural society, that is why the relatives of an offender—and even his teachers—are also punished. The assumption is that if he were taught in a serious way, then, as a son or as a student, he would be unable to misbehave. Therefore, any litigation is shameful, because it indicates a lack of proper education.

Settling disputes in villages is actually part of the educational process that goes on in rural society. I have been asked to attend meetings where I was to help mediate quarrels. In the villagers' view, it was very natural that I should be invited to do so. I am a teacher. Therefore, I read books. Therefore, I must understand rituals. Therefore, I must be an authority in this respect. The other mediators were the village elders. One of the most interesting things about these meetings was that the *baozhang*, the government's representative in the village, never spoke. And the reason he did not speak was that he had no social status in the village at all. He was just a petty bureaucrat. What we now call "mediation" (*tiaojie*) used to be called "critical reasoning" (*pingli*). In almost every meeting of this sort, the same extremely articulate local notable would speak first. His procedure would be first to scold both sides in the dispute. He would say something like this: "This incident is making our *entire* village lose face! Admit your wrongs and go home." Then he would give them a lecture. Sometimes, in a fit of temper, he would even pound on the table. He would tell them what he thought they "should" do. This kind of procedure was very effective, and often both sides in the dispute would be reconciled on the spot. Sometimes they would be penalized and would have to treat all the mediators to an expensive meal. On those occasions, I often felt as if I were watching a referee in a soccer game, blowing his whistle and doling out his penalties.

I remember one especially interesting case. The case involved an old man who was addicted to opium. The eldest son hated his father's habit because it was depleting the family's wealth, but the son could not easily interfere. The second son had no regular employment, and he secretly smoked opium as well. In fact, he would often get his father to smoke opium, so that he could join. The dispute arose when the elder brother recognized what the younger brother was doing, and severely beat him. The younger brother, however, blamed his father, and in a fit of temper, the eldest son scolded the father as well. These mutual recriminations led to a big fight in the family. Eventually, the dispute came before the village elders for resolution. That same gentleman once again spoke first, saying that this scandal involved the entire village. Then he used a range of moral principles to reach a resolution: The younger son should be driven out of the village; he was morally bankrupt, and even from his appearance, one would see that he was up to no good. The eldest son should be fined because he scolded his father. The old man, the father, is the one who received the lecture, because he did not know how to instruct either son in appropriate behavior, and besides that he smoked opium. After the punishments were meted out, everyone went home. That old gentleman who mediated the case later complained to me that each generation is worse than the previous one and that public morality is deteriorating by the day.

Confucius said: "In hearing litigation, I am like any other person. What is necessary, however, is to cause the people to have no litigation."[2] At that moment, after seeing how rural society resolves its disputes, I understood what Confucius meant.

Modern urban society emphasizes individual rights. Rights are not to be violated. The state should protect those rights, and that is the reason modern states have so many laws. Judges in these societies do not dwell on moral issues or ethical concepts. It is not their job to teach morality and ethics to people. The purpose of punishment is not to warn others against following a bad example, but to protect individual rights and to provide for public safety. Especially in civil law, judges do not decide who is right and who is wrong; instead, they determine the rights of the individuals in each case. The British and American legal systems are based on legal precedent. Many times, the aim of a lawsuit is to establish a precedent for people to follow. In a changing society, rules have to change. The environment changes, so mutually negotiated rights have to change as well. In reality, no two cases represent exactly the same situation, so it is often problematic to locate individual rights in a consistent way. Therefore, legal cases are sometimes put forward in order to establish a precedent. These are called "test cases." Proposing such cases presents no inherent moral problem.

Modern society does not view laws as fixed rules. Laws have to follow the times, so the contents of laws have to change. People living in modern society are not all expected to be familiar with laws that constantly change. If they do not know a law, they are not considered "morally bankrupt." Because lawyers must keep abreast of changing laws, they have become an indispensable professional group in modern society.

China is changing from a rural to modern society. However, because most people cling to the old ideas about litigation, it is unlikely that a modern judicial system will be able to take firm hold. First of all, the principles of the modern laws currently in force come from the West and greatly differ from the concepts embodied in the old ethical doctrines. In a previous chapter, I said

2. *Analects*, Book 12, chap. 13.

that the Chinese traditional patterns of a differential mode of association undermined the possibility that a general rule could be
applied to all people. The current laws, however, presume individual equality. This presumption is something not easily understood
by common people. They also have no knowledge of how to use
the processes of the judicial system. Common people from rural
areas are still afraid of taking any case to court, but now China's
new judicial system is beginning to spread to the countryside. Those
people who have been excluded from consideration in rural communities, because of their immoral behavior, now find in this imported legal system new protections. If they do not like what the
village mediators decide, they can always file a lawsuit in the judicial department. In theory, this would be a good thing because it
might destroy the traditions of rural society and put China on the
path toward modernization. In reality, the people who file cases in
the courts are the same people recognized in the countryside as
being morally bankrupt. If you judge them according to current
laws (ignoring, for the moment, any corruption in the legal system), the results often differ from a judgment based on local tradition. What rural people recognize as improper behavior may, in
fact, be perfectly legal. Therefore, from a rural perspective, the
modern judicial system has become an institution that shelters
evildoers.

A county magistrate who concurrently served as a judge told
me about a case that he was hearing. In this case, a man who discovered that his wife was sleeping with another man had beaten
up that man. In rural areas, beating up someone like this is justice.
But adultery is not a crime; besides, there was no proof. Assault
and battery, however, are crimes. The magistrate asked me how
he should judge the case. He knew that if the adulterer were an
honest person, he would never have come to the district head-
quarters to file charges against the husband who had beaten him.
However, those people who have no moral values and who possess only a little legal knowledge could do evil things in the villages, and the law had to protect them. I admitted that this was
probably a common occurrence. The current judicial system has
very distinctive side effects in rural areas. It is destroying the original order based on a rule of rituals, but it has not been able to
establish an effective order based on law. We cannot establish a

social order based on a rule of law simply by making a few legal texts available and by setting up a few courts. More important is how people use these facilities. What is more, the first thing needed is to reform the social structure and the ideological perspective. If there are no reforms in these areas, then simply taking laws and courts to the countryside will not provide any of the advantages of a society ruled by law. Instead, it will only generate those disadvantages associated with having destroyed a society ruled through rituals.

10

An Inactive Government

Scholars who analyze political power can be divided into two groups, each with a different perspective. One group emphasizes social conflict; the other, social cooperation. Depending on the emphasis, what the two see as the nature of political power is quite different.

Those who emphasize a social conflict perspective see political power as the outcome of a struggle between unequally ranked groups and classes. Let us call this kind of power "dictatorial power." Those who come out on top are the ones who have power, and they use their power to dominate those beneath them. They give orders and, through their will, dictate the actions of the dominated. According to this view, the exercise of political power is a continuation of the process of conflict and represents merely a truce, a temporary equilibrium in a continuing struggle. Although the use of military force has ended, contention does not disappear. The vanquished merely recognize their defeat and act more obediently. However, they will not willingly accept the conditions dictated by their victors and will not sincerely submit to their rule. Therefore, political power emerges from the relationship between contending parties. It is the necessary means to maintain the relationship; it is inherently oppressive and works to differentiate the rulers from the ruled. From this perspective, the government apparatus and the institutions of the state are the tools of the dominators. Following this line of reasoning, one can say that government and the state structure itself exist only insofar as they are a part of the process of class struggle. If, one day, the problem of class struggle were solved and societies were no longer divided into classes, then, like leaves in the autumn, government and state institutions would, of their own accord, fall away.

Those who look at power from the perspective of social cooperation see it in quite a different light. The result of a division of labor in society is that everyone is mutually interdependent. The divi-

sion of labor benefits everyone, because it is the basis of the economy. People can achieve more with less labor. Labor represents
both capital and people's sweat. With a division of labor, people
reduce their burdens and increase their enjoyment in life. Enjoyment is certainly what people want, but one cannot be self-reliant
and hope to attain it. One cannot just care for oneself and cannot
just "mind one's own business" (*xianshi*). If others fail to do their
fair share of work, or if they fail to do it well, your own life will be
influenced. Thus, for your own sake, you have to interfere with
others. Similarly, if you fail to do your part, you will influence
other people, and they will interfere with you. In this way, rights
and obligations are generated. Interfering in other people's business is your right; allowing them to interfere in yours is your obligation. Each person has the responsibility to work, as well as the
responsibility to supervise others. People cannot just seek their own
happiness and do whatever they please. They have to perform the
work that society has assigned to them.

But what ensures that this work will be done? What would happen if someone decided not to go along with all of this? At this
point, we see that power arises from a common will. The basis of
this power is social contract and mutual consent. The more complicated the division of labor, the more extensive this power becomes. If you do not want to be constrained by this form of power,
you will have to return to an environment that allows self-reliance.
To be truly independent, you will have to be your own Robinson
Crusoe. Or perhaps you can live in Laotse's ideal state, "a small
nation with few people," and so not feel the weight of so much
power. To put the matter more clearly, you will have to give up
your economic beliefs, forgo the enjoyment you get out of your
possessions, and return to an original state of nature, to a living
standard like that of the storybook hero Tarzan of the Apes. Otherwise, you will never escape the reach of this power, a kind of
power that might best be called "consensual power," a sort of power
that arises out of mutual agreements.

Both the conflict and the cooperative perspectives on power are
grounded in reality and are not actually contradictory. In all human societies, both types of power exist. Although regimes may
differ in the degree to which the two types of power are present,
rulers and their governments represent both types of power si-

multaneously. In a period of social transformation, therefore, it is not easy to have only cooperation and no conflict. At least, that is the lesson we learn from history. The two processes—conflict and cooperation—often overlap and intermix. Conflict contains elements of cooperation, and cooperation contains elements of conflict. Neither is pure. Therefore, the two kinds of power differ more in concept than in reality. To understand the power structure of a community, we have to analyze how the two types of power interrelate. Some communities emphasize one sort of power over the other, while other communities do the reverse. Moreover, in any one community, one type of power relations may come into being among certain people, and the other among other people. For instance, on the surface, people in the United States emphasize consensual power, but, in reality, a sort of dictatorial power still characterizes the relations between the races.

Some people think that power itself is the temptation, that human beings are intrinsically "power hungry." This view overlooks the fact that power is a tool. Although those who hold power may sometimes be driven by a pure desire to dominate or by sadistic psychological perversions, these situations are, after all, abnormal. What people love most are the benefits that flow from power. If power did not bring benefits or if those benefits could be obtained without holding power, the temptation of power would not be so strong. For instance, an opinion poll in England shows that only a small percentage of the people want their children to become members of Parliament or the Cabinet. People in both positions in England have low salaries, even though they do obtain many social rewards. Most people are not in a hurry to get those kinds of lofty positions.

The main temptation of power is to gain economic advantage. From a consensus perspective, people in power do not hold power because they want to protect their own special interests. Instead, they hold power because society needs to reward them with prestige and high pay in order to solicit their services.[1] From a perspective of dictatorial power, however, the relation between power and

1. This reference is to the "functional theory of stratification." For an outline of this theory, see Kingsley Davis and Wilbert Moore, "Some Principles of Stratification," *American Sociological Review* 10 (April 1945): 242–49.

economic advantage is more direct: Rulers use force to maintain their positions, and one of their reasons for doing so is certainly to gain economic advantages. Conversely, without the likelihood of economic advantage, dictatorial power would have little meaning, and therefore would be less likely to occur.

If group A wants to control group B to gain some economic advantage, there must be a precondition—namely, that group B is able to provide this advantage. The production of group B must exceed its consumption so that it has a surplus that makes group A's conquest of it worthwhile. This is very important. A person who produces only enough for his own survival does not make a very good slave. What I am trying to point out here are the limitations of dictatorial power in an agricultural society. When I was doing a survey among Yao tribes in the mountainous regions of Guangxi province, I often noticed that ethnic Chinese people (*han-ren*) had occupied the land of the Yao but had never enslaved them. There were certainly a lot of reasons for this; but in my view, the major one was that the place was just too poor, and those Yao tribesmen who planted rice fields could not lower their standard of living yet further to become tenants of the Han Chinese. Therefore, when the Chinese won a battle with one of the Yao tribes, the Yao just gave up their land and moved. In wars in agrarian societies, the most common pattern is to drive out the natives, take over their land, and cultivate it personally. This especially happens when a population is large, labor is plentiful, and the available arable land is being fully utilized. In studying Chinese history, we often come across references to conquerors who "buried tens of thousands of enemies alive." In fact, until quite recently, it was not unusual to encounter groups of roving bandits who would kill people with great ferocity. Such a situation is not one that an aggressive industrial power could understand.[2]

---

2. In the 1986 reissue (Xianggang: Sanlian shudian), pp. 67–68, Fei cut the remainder of this paragraph. The original paragraph, in the 1947 reissue (Shanghai: Shanghai guanchashe), pp. 67–68, ends as follows: "Killing people with abandon, mowing them down like grass, is often seen to be a characteristic of Asian cruelty. If that really is a characteristic of Asians, it is not a genetic one; it does not run in their blood. Instead, it is a characteristic of the place and not of the people. On barren soil, a toiling laborer can only support himself. He lacks value that can be utilized. If another group conquers such people who have no surplus value, they have to kill them, bury them alive, or drive them away. The conquest would be

I do not mean to imply that a dictatorial power cannot be established in an agricultural society. On the contrary, it is precisely this kind of society that produces a foundation for imperial power, but that is because rural society does not possess organizations capable of mounting resistance to this form of government. The historical record is very clear; nomadic invaders have repeatedly overrun agricultural societies, and the agricultural plains of East Asia have always endured empires of one sort or another. However, agrarian empires are not good examples of dictatorial power holding. In fact, they are relatively weak governments. Imperial power is unable to develop great strength, because the social and economic foundations are simply insufficient to support a powerful dictatorial power. The population increases daily, and accordingly the agricultural surplus decreases daily. Even the peace supplied by successful agrarian empires provides further opportunities for population increases.

Chinese history is proof of this fact. Ambitious emperors, anxious to open new frontiers, will build cities and dig rivers. Normally, such rulers would not be considered tyrants but would be thought of as great leaders making an investment for a nation's future, such as Franklin Roosevelt was with his Tennessee Valley Authority. But an agrarian economy like China's does not produce enough surplus to finance such large projects easily, and without sufficient surplus large public-works projects always cause great discontent—so much so that people will try to escape imperial control. Therefore, active emperors simultaneously burden their subjects with taxation and strengthen their control over them. Both tasks in turn add to their expenses. Suddenly, individuals like Chen Sheng and Wu Guang will rise up in rebellion, and there will be great upheavals everywhere.[3] Such rebellions will claim the lives of many people, thereby easing population pressures. The chaos will end, and peace will prevail once again. At this juncture, peo-

---

meaningless if the conquerors allowed the defeated to continue farming. In this sense, conquest actually means to conquer the land, not the people. Killing people and grabbing their land is the normal mode of conquest in agrarian societies. East Asia is an area with a large population but little arable lands that are not already fully utilized. Under these circumstances, the value of human life is regarded as extremely low. Cruelty is a consequence of the economy."

3. Chen Sheng and Wu Guang are famous leaders of peasant rebellions at the end of the Qin dynasty (221–207 B.C.).

ple want to do nothing more than rest. Imperial power will also seek nothing; it will simply be inactive. Through their own inaction, the rulers, as the saying goes, will "nourish the people." After a period of recuperation, the imperial government will gradually accumulate greater resources, and the emperors' ambitions will grow again. The cycle will thus begin anew.

In order to maintain their power, imperial rulers draw upon the experiences of their predecessors. They find survival value in doing nothing, and they glorify this strategy by establishing *wuwei zhengzhi*, an inactive government, a government at peace with its people.

Dictatorships have economic restraints. In China, the distance between the ruler and his subjects is characterized by the saying "Heaven is high and the emperor is far away." With this kind of gap between the ruler and the ruled, those rulers who seem to exercise dictatorial powers really rule by allowing people in rural society to manage their own affairs. Power in rural society is primarily consensual power, but this kind of power is also limited by economic conditions. As I have already said, the consensual power grows out of a division of labor and is able to expand only when the division of labor itself develops. Rural society is a small-scale peasant economy, and, if necessary, each peasant household can become self-sufficient, except for a few items of daily necessity. The household may simply close its doors on the larger economy. When this occurs, we can imagine that the scope of consensual power would also decrease. Judging from the reality of people's lives in agrarian societies, then, we can see that the power structure, although it may be labeled a "dictatorship," is actually loose, weak, and nominal. It is a government that does not actively govern at all.

11

Rule by Elders

To understand the power structure in rural society, one needs to go beyond the two concepts of power that I discussed in the previous chapter—dictatorial power and consensual power. We may use our understanding of the nature of rural societies as a means to explain the actual limitations of authoritarian governments in agrarian societies. But demonstrating these limitations does not lead us to infer that the power structure of rural society is somehow "democratic." Democracy is a form of consensual power. In a traditional agrarian society, although government rule may be dictatorial at the top, the force of that power does not penetrate rural areas to any great extent. In rural areas, government is very inactive, is really very weak. The relative absence of government in rural areas, however, does not then mean that local society becomes a place full of "citizens" possessing equal rights and jointly participating in their governance.

There is some controversy about the nature of Chinese local politics. Some people say that, although China does not have political democracy, it does have a sort of social democracy. Others say that in the Chinese political structure we can identify two layers, a non-democratic and a democratic layer, with the former on top and the latter on the bottom. There is some truth in both views. But I cannot say that either is correct, for the simple reason that there is another kind of power that is neither dictatorial nor consensual, a kind of power that arises from neither conflict nor cooperation. Instead, this kind of power emerges in the process of establishing an orderly succession in society, a kind of social reproduction, by which social power and privilege are passed from one generation to the next. A succession of this kind rests on power generated through education and through patriarchal privilege, or what is normally called "paternalism."

"Social reproduction" is a term I coined in my book *Systems of*

Reproduction, but it is really not a new concept. It refers to a process of social metabolism. Life and death are capricious; the length of a person's life is always limited. The world is only a hotel in which one stays for a while; whether the stay is long or short does not make much difference. However, the rules in this hotel are more complicated and strict than those in actual hotels. No newcomer understands the rules before entering the door. Moreover, those who enter the hotel do not do so by their own choice, and, once in, they cannot freely leave. There is only one hotel and no more. True, this hotel is large and has many sections; each section has a different culture with distinctive rules. The only similarity among sections is that they all have rules. They post on the wall their "Notice to the Guests," which seems to contain more than ten commandments. Those who live in this hotel have to receive an education; they have to know the rules well enough so that they can fully satisfy their desires without bumping up against the limits of what is possible.

Some of the rules in the society result from social conflicts, and others from social cooperation. Therefore, the limits of individual behavior in any particular setting are set by both dictatorial and consensual powers. But, regardless of how they are established, these are rules that demand people's understanding and compliance. If human beings were like ants and bees, things would be simpler. The rules of group life would be anchored in biology, so to master them would require no education. Human rules, however, are all human made. To pick up tofu gracefully with chopsticks and to dance in high heels without stepping on your partner's feet are not easy things to do. If you won't learn or if you won't practice, you cannot do these things correctly. And when you are learning to do them, you cannot fear the difficulties or dread the trouble. But fearing difficulties and dreading trouble are only natural. Therefore, learning requires some form of compulsion, and behind this compulsion there must be some form of power.

This kind of power is neither consensual nor dictatorial. It would be an exaggeration to say that we are entering into a social contract when we require our children to wear shoes outdoors. Social contracts presuppose the exercise of individual will. Individuals do not have the right to break the terms of their contract freely, but in the process of setting the terms of a contract, the free will of each individual needs to be respected. A democracy, therefore, is a form of government that combines both individual will and social compulsion. However, the process of education does not give rise to this kind of problem. The one who is being educated has no opportunity to exercise choice. What such a person learns is what we call *wenhua*, or culture itself. Culture exists before the individual. We Chinese do not use the term *will* in reference to a child's personality, because the process of education does not require that a child's will be recognized. Actually, what we call "will" is not like a biological organ that develops gradually over time. And it is not a psychological phenomenon either. Rather, it is a social product, an object of social recognition. "Will" is an essential element in the maintenance of a consensual order, but not of other orders. That we do not recognize a "will" in nonadults proves that they have not yet entered a situation where order is assumed to be consensually based.

I said in my earlier book *Systems of Reproduction*, "Children come into a world that is made not for their convenience, but rather for that of adults. They enter the world with neither a capacity to establish a new order nor a desire to comply with the old order."[1] In teaching children how to live in society, those doing the teaching neither seek nor consider the advice and consent of the children they teach. We can certainly say that this process is undemocratic, but we cannot say it is dictatorial. Dictatorial power develops in the course of social conflicts and is a tool that rulers use to maximize their exploitation of the ruled. It is an overstatement, therefore, to say that the process of education is exploitative. I once wrote that raising and educating children is the sort of job that "harms the self, even as it benefits others." Except, perhaps, for a sense of spiritual fulfillment, what benefit does one get out of raising an embryo to an adult? There may be some exploitation when young children are treated as adults. But, at a minimum, having children in order to benefit from them economically is likely a losing proposition.

As I have written, it appears at first glance that "the amount of correction a child gets in one hour would exceed the criticism an

---

1. Fei's reference: *Shengyu zhidu* [Shanghai: Shangwu, 1947], p. 101.

adult would receive in one year. To be a citizen under the most tyrannical king is no worse than being a child with the most loving parents."[2] In fact, however, a strict father and a tyrannical king differ in that the parents substitute for society itself in the process of education. They teach the child how to mold his or her self according to established cultural patterns, and how to manage the social roles embedded in group life. The goal of this educational process is, on the one hand, for the benefit of society and, on the other hand, for the benefit of the person being educated. But either way, it is not a relationship that can be characterized as one of domination.

The power differential that arises as part of the process of education is most obvious in the parent-child relationship, but it is not restricted to that relationship. All cultural, as opposed to political, coercion partakes of this kind of power. The difference between culture and politics lies here: cultural norms are readily accepted because they are already taken for granted by the society; politics, however, operate in the absence of a set of agreed-upon norms, when there are all sorts of different competing opinions about how to act and when short-term solutions to problems are sought. Unlike politics, the cultural foundation of a society is necessarily consensual, but to those new members of society, learning culture is a compulsory educational process.

In a relatively static society, culture is stable. There are very few new problems. Living consists primarily of following a set of traditional recipes. In a society completely regulated by tradition, there would be no politics, just education. Although such a society does not actually exist, rural society comes close. The simplicity of political action in our society is described in the sayings "To govern is to say little" (*Wei zheng bu zai duo yan*) and "To rule is to do nothing" (*Wuwei er zhi*). In this kind of society, human behavior is regulated by traditional rituals. Confucians were always interested in supporting a ruler who would base his power on the educational process, but they were never enthusiastic about maintaining a social order based on dictatorial powers. "Tyranny," they wrote, "is fiercer than a tiger." The proper way to rule, they said, is "to rule

2. Fei's reference: *Shengyu zhidu*, p. 101.

through ethics." The idea is carried further in the saying that pre-
scribes how government officials are supposed to act: "Be parents
to the people." This idea represents patriarchalism in China.

The extension of educational power to relationships among adults
requires a stable culture. A stable cultural tradition provides a
guarantee of efficacy. If we seek specific solutions for specific problems, we must, as the saying goes, "Even into old age, live and
learn." Problems in each stage of life are different. Culture is like
an almanac to which we constantly turn for guidance as new problems arise. In such a society, there is no dividing line, no entry
point into adulthood, that puts a person beyond instruction.
Everyone who is older than I must have come across the problems
I encounter. Therefore, elders can be my "teachers." If three individuals walk together, one of them must be capable of teaching me
how to deal with my problems. Every older person possesses the
power to teach, and thereby to impose a culture upon, every younger
person. Confucius even taught this. "Respect your elder brother,"
he said. That is, when you meet someone older, you must respect
and submit to that person's educational power.

It is not an accident that, when we greet guests, we ask their
age. Such politeness shows that, in our society, the way we treat
each other is related to a social order based on seniority. The ranking by seniority also demonstrates the effectiveness of power gained
through education. Seniority is an extremely important principle
in the way we address one another. We distinguish an elder brother
from a younger brother, an elder sister from a younger sister, an
uncle who is older than our father from one who is younger. Many
other societies do not have these distinctions at all. I remember that
my teacher Dr. Shirokogoroff once reminded me that the distinction between the senior and the junior is the most fundamental
principle in the Chinese kinship system. Sometimes it even over-
rides the generational principle.[3] Kinship principles are formed in
the midst of social life. The importance of the principle of seniority
in Chinese society indicates the importance of education and of the
power that arises from education.

3. For a discussion of the principles underlying hierarchy in Chinese lineages,
see Hugh Baker, *Chinese Family and Kinship* (New York: Columbia University Press,
1979).

When culture is unstable and when traditional methods are inadequate to solve current problems, educational power becomes restricted to the relationships between parents and children and between teachers and students, and lasts for a shorter period. In the process of social change, people cannot rely on experience for guidance. Instead, they must rely on abstract principles, principles that go beyond specific situations. Those who develop and use such principles are not necessarily older people. After all, competence of this sort is not closely related to age. It is related mainly to intelligence and expertise—and also to opportunity. And in reference to opportunity, younger people may have more chances to show their competence than older people, because they are less afraid of change; they are curious and willing to experiment.

In periods of social transition, habits limit one's ability to adapt to change. In such times, it is obstinate and backward-looking to use past experiences as a measure of present actions. Such obstinacy and backwardness are not merely foolish and humorous at times, but are a threat to survival under the changed circumstances. If a child calls his father by a nickname, he will not risk being scolded for being informal. Quite the contrary, this expression of intimacy will give the father the comfort of not being pushed aside. When respect is not based on age, comparing who is senior and who is junior becomes a meaningless exercise; people will stop asking about each other's age when they first meet. This kind of society is far removed from rural society.

Now let us return to China's rural society. Its structure of power contains elements of both dictatorial and consensual power; but, besides these, the structure of power rests upon education. This power generated in the process of education is neither democratic nor dictatorial; it differs from both. Therefore, if you measure Chinese society by the standards of Western concepts of democracy, there will be some similarities, but it will not be exactly the same. Such comparisons are inaccurate, for the terms do not apply. If another term were really required to characterize the power structure in Chinese, then I could not suggest anything better than "rule by elders" (*zhanglao tongzhi*).

12

Consanguinity and Regionalism

In a static culture, substantial social differences appear between people who differ only in age. The older people wield imposing power over the younger. This is the foundation of a consanguineous society. Consanguinity (*xueyuan*) means that people's rights and obligations are determined by kinship. Kinship is the relationship constituted through reproduction and marriage. Strictly speaking, consanguinity only defines the relatedness that derives from reproduction, from the parent-child relationship. And in truth, in a society having a patrilineal kinship organization, kinship derived through reproduction is valued much more highly than that derived through marriage, so much so that we can call such a society consanguineous.

Reproduction is necessary for social continuity. This is true for all societies. What differs, however, is that in some societies a person's social position derives from relationships that are fixed by the fact of procreation, while in others this form of relatedness is less important. The former society is consanguineous. Generally speaking, consanguineous societies are stable and static. It is difficult for a society undergoing frequent changes to remain consanguineous. Social stability suggests a lack of structural changes; even though individuals change position within the structure, the structure itself remains motionless. People are limited by their fate, by the circumstance of their birth; they continue in life as long as they can, and then they die. The consanguineous society maintains structural stability by using the biological process underlying reproduction as the medium to establish social continuity. The principle is that when the father dies, the son succeeds. A farmer's son becomes a farmer, and a merchant's son becomes a merchant; such successions in occupation are consanguineous. An aristocrat's son becomes an aristocrat; such succession in identity is consanguineous. A rich man's son becomes rich; such succession in wealth is consanguineous. Up to the present time, very few societies have entirely abandoned all forms of consanguineous succession—such is the power and importance of kinship in the reproductive process. However, if the social structure is changing, it is also impossible for succession to be determined entirely according to consanguinity. Until such time as reproduction is fully socialized, the strength of consanguinity will be determined by rates of social change.

The social positions determined by consanguinity are not subject to individual choice, since the determination of one's parents is sheer chance. It seems irrational that societies should use the circumstance of parentage to decide everyone's occupation, status, and wealth. The only argument for the rationality of this procedure would be that it is the most basic way to stabilize an existing order. Therefore, as long as one accepts the principle of consanguinity (and who, in fact, has ever seriously doubted or explored the reason for the existence of such a principle?), many different kinds of social disputes will simply not occur at all.

Consanguinity is a stabilizing force. In stable societies, a tie to a specific place (*diyuan*), or regionalism, is no more than an extension of consanguinity and cannot be separated from it. "Being born and dying in the same place" fixes the relationship between places and people. Therefore, birth—that is, one's bloodline—determines one's ties to a location. The reproduction of a population across generations resembles sprouts growing out of the same tree trunks; in space, there appear to be clumps of people. This closeness in space reflects the closeness in consanguinity. Geographical location is actually socialized space. We distinguish directions in terms of superiority and inferiority: the left is superior to the right, and the south superior to the north. These are consanguineous coordinates. Space itself is inherently formless, but using our consanguineous coordinates, we divide space into directions and into positions. In fact, the word we use to describe the location of a person in society, "position" (*diwei*), was originally used to indicate a location in "space" (*kongjian*), but gradually the term acquired a social significance as well. This change in meaning should remind us that our association with "a place" (*di*) rests on social relationships.

Those societies where people do not move around much tend to be self-sufficient enough that very little migration is required. Where the population is static, lineage groups actually imply a geographical location. In fact, the concept of village may be superfluous. We have heard the children's song "Row, row, row your boat to grandma's home." From our own experience, we know that "grandma's home" means an enduring relationship to a place. This combination of consanguinity and regionalism is what communities, in their original sense, were all about.

But human beings are, after all, not plants; they will move. Lineage segmentation, that process of "cell division" in rural society, is unavoidable. A constantly reproducing consanguineous group cannot live together in one place for very long. The group needs a certain amount of land for its survival, but the population of the group necessarily grows beyond the capacity of the land nearby to provide for it. When this occurs, the group has to segment geographically, because the distance between where people live and where they farm becomes so great that it hinders their ability to farm. But because a group's landholdings cannot be expanded without limit, what happens in the short run is that existing landholdings are farmed ever more intensively. Such intensive cultivation leads to gradually decreasing productivity, so the group is again restricted by its ability to survive on a given allotment of land. Again the group is forced to divide. The lineage segment that splits off moves to other places to look for land.

If the lineage segment is able to claim some land that has never been worked before and to develop a village community there, it will still maintain its consanguineous connections with the original village, and even name the new place after the old. Its actions would seem to deny that any real separation occurred. This phenomenon is commonplace in societies with many immigrants. If people traveling in the United States just looked at the names of places, they would have the illusion that Europe had been transplanted there. New England and New York are famous examples. Many Londons and many Moscows can be found on the American map. In our own case, however, consanguineous geographical relationships are much more conspicuous. I left my hometown, Wujiang, when I was ten years old, and lived in Suzhou for nine years. Both are in Jiangsu province. But whenever I fill out a form of some kind, I put "Jiangsu, Wujiang" as my native place (*jiguan*). During the recent war, I lived in Yunnan for eight years, but my native place did not change. Even my child, born in Yunnan, inherited my native place. She will probably write "Jiangsu, Wujiang" on all the forms that she fills out throughout her life. My ancestors lived in Wujiang for over twenty generations, but our lanterns bore the big red characters "Jiangxia Fei." Jiangxia is in Hubei province; so, geographically speaking, why should I be connected with Jiangxia? That is the same with my child: on what grounds should she have a geographical connection with Wujiang, a place she has never been to? Obviously, in our rural society, one's geographical location does not create a distinctive identity. Our native place is the same as our father's native place, rather than the place of our birth or the place where we currently live. We inherit a native place just as we inherit a family name; it is like a blood relationship. Therefore, we can conclude that one's native place is only *the projection of consanguinity into space*.

Many people who migrate from their hometowns do not start new villages in other places. Instead, they settle down in other established communities. If these people who have no relatives nearby could organize a local group, this group would be based not on blood relationships but on a current geographical location. In this case, consanguinity and geography would be separated. But this seldom happens in Chinese rural society. In villages in all parts of the country, I often met people who are labeled "guest" (*kebian*), "new guest" (*xinke*), or "outsider" (*waicunren*). Their residential registration cards also indicate that they are "nonnatives" (*jiji*). Modern cities always establish procedures for how people are able to become legal residents, and the main requirement is a certain period of residence. However, in rural villages, the period of residence does not matter. I know many people who have lived in a village for several generations but are still called "new guests."

When I was doing surveys in Jiangcun and in Lucun, I paid close attention to the question "How can one become a native villager?" Generally speaking, the replies suggested that anyone who wanted to be considered a native resident had to fulfill several conditions. The first condition was that the person have "roots" in the earth—that is, own land in the village. The second condition was that he or she enter local kinship circles through marriage. These are not easy conditions to satisfy. The land in rural China cannot be bought and sold freely. The rights over the land are protected by lineages, so it is difficult to sell land to outsiders unless the sale is approved by the lineage groups themselves. Marriage is certainly a way to gain a social connection to a geographical location. When a woman marries a man in a different community and goes to live in his home, she becomes a member of that community. Likewise, if a man marries into the bride's family, he, too, can enter the local community. However, it is not easy for a "guest" to marry a local woman, because such a marriage would allow their children to be considered members of the local community. Perhaps the person needs to own land first before he can more readily enter into the local consanguineous networks. But this is only my hypothesis; I need comparable material from other villages to substantiate it.

The "guest" residents (those who live on the margin of the community) cannot be regarded as having entered the village group, because they often do not have the same rights as the residents. They are not seen as "insiders" and cannot be trusted. I previously wrote that rural society is an intimate society, but here we have people who are "strangers," with an unknown past; so native people are suspicious of them. Nevertheless, because of this very characteristic, "guest" residents find special vocations in rural societies.

The intimacy of close kinship ties limits some kinds of social activities, mainly those requiring conflict or competition. Your relatives and you are from the same blood; you have all sprouted from one root. In principle, you share the same fate; your pains and sorrows are interconnected, and so you should help meet each other's needs. Moreover, living closely and intimately with each other, relatives become, over long periods of time, mutually interdependent in many aspects of their lives. There is no way to count the favors given or received. The unity of the intimate group depends on the fact that each member owes countless favors to the other members. This all seems so obvious to us that we take it for granted. Friends vie with each other to pay bills, each hoping to let the others "owe them one" (*renqing*). Such debts are like an investment to the lender. When you owe another person a favor (*renqing*), you have to look for an opportunity to return a bigger favor. By repaying the favor with a bigger favor, you make others owe you more favors in the future. So it goes, back and forth; the continuing reciprocation maintains the cooperation among people in the group. It is impossible for a person not to owe favors in such an intimate group. In fact, people are afraid to square their accounts (*suanzhang*). To settle accounts (*suanzhang*) or to be completely square (*qingsuan*) with somebody means to break off relationships, because if people do not owe something to each other, there will be no need for further contact.

But no matter how close relatives are to you, they are, after all, not you. Although relatives are concerned with each other, their concern goes only so deep. To maintain the closeness of the group—to ensure that intimacy itself does not turn into resentment—too many favors, too much *renqing*, should be avoided. In social relationships (*shehui guanxi*), rights and obligations must be mutually balanced, although the balancing of the relationship may be spaced out over a long period of time. But if it is one-sided, a social relationship cannot be sustained without some kind of compulsory force. One of the methods to prevent a break in social relationships is to reduce the burdens placed on the relationship itself. For example, in the rural areas of Yunnan province, there are "money clubs" (*qianhui*) called *zhong;* these clubs are a type of cooperative credit association. I investigated the relationship of those people in the *zhong* and found two underlying similarities among members. First, each *zhong* excluded relatives from the same lineage; second, it included friends with whom members had no kinship relationship. I asked why the members did not let people from the same lineage join their *zhong*. The reason they gave is very practical. In theory, people belonging to the same lineage have an obligation to take care of each other's needs and generally to help each other. If kinsmen are able and kind, they will directly loan money to relatives without joining a *zhong*. In truth, such generous relatives are fairly rare. However, if relatives join a *zhong* and do not pay their loans on time, it is difficult to force them to do so because of the members' relationship (*renqing*) with them. These unrepaid loans will cause the *zhong* to fail. For this reason, people trying to start a *zhong* do not recruit members of their own lineage. Other relatives, such as those on the mother's side, may join a *zhong*, but often they do not pay their money on time either. I once interviewed the head of a *zhong* who was worried about exactly this kind of situation. He told me with a sigh that it is best not to be involved with relatives in money matters. His words provide an explanation of what I meant above about lightening the burden on social relations with relatives.

The more developed the society, the more frequent and complex the contacts among people become, and the more difficult it is to maintain a good balance between one's rights and obligations by relying simply on *renqing*, on one's intuitive sense about the appropriate levels of reciprocation between people. Therefore, the need to "settle accounts on the spot" increases. In this context, money becomes both the unit of exchange to settle accounts and the medium of exchange to calculate levels of reciprocation. With money as the unit, the settling of accounts can be exact. And with money as the medium, a balanced credit relationship can be guaranteed. *Renqing* exchanges based on money calculations allow accounts to be cleared; they also bring this aspect of life into the scope of what is normally included in "the economy." In a narrow sense, then, *renqing*-motivated money exchanges become subsumed under the knack of doing business; hence, these aspects of life become commercialized.

Commerce cannot exist in an intimate consanguineous society. Although exchanges do take place in such a society, people exchange with *renqing*, by giving gifts to each other. In essence, both exchanging gifts and exchanging goods for commercial purposes can be used to supply needs. The two differ only in how people settle their accounts. A barter trading system based on large-scale exchanges of presents can still be seen in the Pacific islands. The Kula system that Malinowski described and analyzed is such an example.[1] This system of trade is not only complex but also quite restrictive: trading relationships are usually established among people not connected by ties of consanguinity. In Chinese rural society, there are special markets created for trading. The markets usually are located not in a village but in an open space. People from all over come to this special place and act, as they say, "without human feelings" (*wuqing*). When they trade, people momentarily set aside their original relationships and settle all exchanges

1. The Kula system is an interisland, intertribal trading system found in Melanesia. For a description of Malinowski's work on the Kula system, see Bronislaw Malinowski, *Argonauts of the Western Pacific* (London: George Routledge, 1922).

on the spot. I have often seen neighbors carrying goods to a market ten miles (*li*) away to exchange with each other and then walk the long distance back home again. Why can't they exchange at their front doors? Why should they make such a long trip to the market? The trip has its function. When standing at their own front doors, they are neighbors. But when they are in the market, they are "strangers." The act of settling accounts on the spot should occur only between strangers and should not involve other social relationships.

When an economy becomes more complex and exchanges in periodic markets give way to exchanges in established stores, the position of "guest" provides a special convenience. The outsiders living on the margin of a consanguineous community become the vehicle for business activities. The villagers can bargain with them and square their accounts with them on the spot. Favors are unnecessary, and there is no need to feel embarrassed in bargaining. According to what I have learned, except for some stands run by poor old people who are virtually beggars, most stores in villages are run by the "new guests"—people from outside the village. Here, too, business develops outside of consanguineous relationships.

Regionalism, the geographical tie to a home region, is a social relationship that has developed out of commerce. Blood ties provide the foundation for status in Chinese society, but regional ties provide the foundation for contractual obligations. Contract here means the agreement reached between strangers. When making contracts, people exercise their freedom of choice. In carrying out their contracts, people rely both on the trustworthiness of the parties and on the law. If laws are to be effective, they must be supported by the consensual power of the people. To fulfill the conditions of a contract is to settle accounts—to take complete care of the rights and obligations as required by the terms of the contract. This requires careful calculation, an exact unit of exchange, and a reliable medium of exchange. Calm thinking is involved, not personal emotion. Reason dominates contractual activities. These are special features of modern society, and they are exactly what rural society lacks.

Changing from a society linked together through blood ties to a society integrated on the basis of geographical location is a qualitative, historically momentous social transformation.

13

Separating Names from Reality

It is convenient to regard rural society as basically static, especially when we contrast it with modern society. But, in fact, no society is entirely static. Rural society simply changes more slowly than modern society. Although slow, the pace of change in rural society is indicative of something more. Different rates of change may indicate different types of change. In this chapter, I am going to discuss the type of change that occurs in the slow transformation of rural society.

When I discussed the nature of power, I proposed three types: dictatorial power growing out of social conflict; consensual power growing out of social cooperation; and paternalistic power growing out of generational succession. Now I want to propose a fourth type, which occurs in periods of rapid social transition. The term *generational succession* indicates individual mobility in a society with a fixed social structure. The term *social transition* indicates changes in the social structure itself. The two processes of change are not necessarily in conflict but, rather, can coexist. No society would suddenly one day turn up with an entirely different social structure. No matter how fast the transition was, it would still be gradual. Whatever changes occur in a given period of time, they always pertain only to a small part of the whole social structure. Therefore, the two types of power that grow out of the two social processes necessarily exist simultaneously. But they are inversely related; as one wanes, the other waxes. If society changes slowly, paternalistic power is stronger; if it changes rapidly, a different phenomenon occurs, which is characterized by the saying "Fathers do not act like fathers, and sons do not act like sons" (*fu bu fu, zi bu zi*). Therefore, when rapid changes occur, the paternalistic power of fathers over sons diminishes accordingly.

A social structure itself has no inherent need to change. Some scholars, including one I mentioned earlier, Oswald Spengler, view social structure (which they see as a major component of culture) as an organic being that, like our bodies, has a life cycle. In youth, it is strong; in old age, it is weak. I am not willing to accept this view, for social structure, like other parts of culture, is produced by people; it is a tool used by people in society to satisfy their needs. Changes in a social structure occur when the social structure no longer meets people's needs, and people want it to change. It is like writing characters with a brush. A brush and Chinese characters are tools, and we use them to convey meanings to others. If, however, we want to convey our ideas to English people, then Chinese characters and a brush are no longer effective tools; we would have to use other tools, such as the English language and typewriters.

Social changes often occur when the old structure can no longer cope with new circumstances. When people first encounter a new set of circumstances, they discover that the old methods are not effective in bringing about expected results. As a consequence, difficulties creep into life. People will not give up the old methods before they find them clearly inadequate. The old ways of life have their inertia. But if old methods no longer meet people's needs, people will eventually begin to distrust them. On the one hand, holding on to ineffective tools is senseless and inconvenient and may even result in losses. On the other hand, new methods are not ready-made but have to be invented by someone, or learned from some other culture, or otherwise imported. And then the new methods have to be tested, and only afterward will people begin to accept them. Then the process of social transition comes to an end. During the transitional period, people will feel perplexed and at a loss. They will be full of tension, hesitant, and uneasy. It is at this juncture that a type of person whom we might call "a cultural hero" (*wenhua yingxiong*) most likely appears. This person is able to provide the way to organize new procedures and to gain people's trust. This kind of person, at this point at least, may dominate followers; therefore, a certain power accrues to him. This power differs from dictatorial power, because it is not based on an exploitative relationship. It also differs from consensual power, because it is not bestowed by society. It differs from paternalistic power as well, because it is not based on tradition. It is produced by changing trends; it is a power brought on by changing times; therefore, I will call it "temporal power" (*shishi quanli*).[1]

Temporal power can be found in primitive societies. In such societies, people often encounter unusual situations, and they need capable people to provide solutions. Such people are regarded as heroes. Wars are also special circumstances, and in times of war heroes become prominent. In modern times, society is rapidly changing; accordingly, this type of power is gaining momentum again. It is interesting to see that temporal power shows up most clearly when a backward society is undergoing rapid modernization. I think we can look at the nature of power in the Soviet Union from this perspective. British and American scholars think it is a type of dictatorial power, because in form it is a dictatorship. But from the standpoint of the people in the Soviet Union, this dictatorship is different from czarism. If we adopt the concept of temporal power, it may be easier for us to understand its nature.

This power is least advanced in stable societies. Insofar as its social structure meets people's daily needs, Chinese rural society is among the most stable of societies. It has few "leaders" and few "heroes." Stability is, of course, relative; but it is safe to say that change here is very slow. But just using the phrase "very slow" is not very clear; we should also ask exactly how slow. Confucius has already provided an answer to this question: "Nothing should be changed until three years after your father dies." In other words, social change becomes absorbed into the regular cycle of generational succession. This is, indeed, a sign of a stable society.

The concept of filial piety that Confucian scholars stress is actually a way to maintain social stability. Filial piety means that there should be no disobedience. This concept recognizes the priority of paternalistic power. The most senior people represent the tradition. If you comply with the tradition, you will not disobey your father's instructions. The representatives of this tradition will die,

---

1. The type of power that Fei is describing here, which is awkwardly called "temporal power," is similar to Max Weber's "charismatic domination." Fei's treatment of this kind of power is fairly rudimentary in this chapter. For Weber's discussion of charismatic domination, see *Economy and Society*, ed. Guenther Roth and Claus Wittich (2 vols.) (Berkeley: University of California Press, 1978), chap. 14.

and you yourself will become senior to others; it is merely a matter of time. If the speed of social change is as slow as the speed of generational succession, then parents and children, representing two different generations, will have no conflicts. Tradition itself changes gradually, and therefore can support the leadership of older people. A society of this kind does not need a "revolution."

From a societal point of view, if the leaders can keep up with the pace of social change, society may avoid the turmoil caused by a larger social transformation. England is a good example. Many people envy the fact that it was able to carry out many fundamental reforms without bloodshed. But these same people overlook the conditions that enabled the British to do so. In the past few centuries, Great Britain has been a world leader, and it is the country where the industrial revolution began. In British society, the ruling class is also the class that can best adapt to a changing environment. The ability of that class to adapt to change matched the pace of change in that environment, so that a bloody revolution was unnecessary. Whether Great Britain can keep this record depends on whether it can maintain this coordination.

Rural society has a fixed environment. If a son can wait three years after his father dies to begin to make changes, then whatever social changes are made will likely not give rise to much conflict. In the world of human affairs, the oldest people maintain their power, and the youngest, holding to the standard of "no disobedience," accept the rule of tradition. There is no active opposition here; besides, the paternalistic power of the elders would tolerate no opposition. Paternalistic power is based on education, the transferal of knowledge from the knowledgeable to the ignorant. If the cultural knowledge passed on is useful, there is no need for the learner to oppose the teacher. If the cultural knowledge passed on is useless, education itself becomes totally meaningless, but opposition still does not arise in this relationship between senior and junior.

Opposition is tolerated, and even encouraged, only where there is consensual power. Because consensual power is based on contract, the power holders are closely watched to see whether they comply with the contract. Moreover, opposition—that is, disagreement—is the first step in achieving agreement. Under dictatorial power, there is no open opposition, only passive resistance. The relationship between ruler and ruled presupposes opposition, and thus dictatorial power is required in the first place to suppress any resistance. With temporal power, opposition occurs when there are different solutions to the same problems. Sometimes a society cannot experiment with different schemes at the same time, so disputes occur among the different advocates. These disputes may lead to a "cold war," with each advocate engaged in a propaganda battle to win over the people. Each person, seeking the success of his own scheme, feels that the other schemes distract people's attention and divert support that he needs in order to prevail. Hence, there emerges an intolerance toward others and an attempt at total ideological control. The main thrust of such ideological struggle is to win over opposing alignments, and when such an intolerance occurs, opposition becomes confrontational.

Let us look again at Chinese rural society, a society ruled by the paternalistic power of elders. In this type of society, opposition to what the elders say takes the form of an "interpretation." Such interpretations outwardly maintain the form of paternalistic power but change the content. Except for the Warring States period (480–221 B.C.), when society went through a great social transformation, Chinese intellectual history has followed Confucianism as its primary authority. People have had to justify social change by reinterpreting the old authorities. Such reinterpretations lead to a widening separation between the names of phenomena and their reality. With paternalistic power, people are not allowed to oppose traditional forms. But as long as they pay lip service to the form, they may reinterpret and thereby change the content. The consequence of this practice is inevitable. We say one thing but mean another. People who have grown up in old-style Chinese families all understand how the interpretation of paternal will can be distorted to maintain the facade of "no disobedience." Under such circumstances, hypocrisy is not only unavoidable; it is a necessity. Unable to oppose the impracticable doctrines and orders issued by the elders, one simply distorts their wishes while giving them face—that is, outward compliance. The gap between the name and underlying reality, however, increases as the pace of social change intensifies. This gap would not develop in a social structure that is totally static, but a totally static social structure does not exist. In a paternalistic social structure, during times of little social change, elders will not tolerate opposition. As the speed of change accelerates, a gap emerges between what the elders demand and what others are actually able to do. Distorted interpretations become commonplace. Position and power, name and substance, words and deeds, theory and reality—all tend to separate and lose their interconnectedness.

14

From Desire to Necessity

My previous discussion of temporal power makes me think of an additional dimension of social change. This dimension is implied in a set of terms that we now hear used a lot, terms such as *social planning* and, even more extreme, *social engineering*. Obviously, such terms have a modern meaning that is unfamiliar in a rural society. They indicate that a profound change has occurred in the way people think about their society. We must examine this change in perception if we want to understand the differences between temporal and patriarchal power.

Humans have discovered that society can be planned. This is a great discovery. It demonstrates that humans have already departed from their rural roots, since such an idea simply could not exist in a truly rural society. In rural society, people are able to use their desires (*yuwang*) as the means to guide their activities. But in modern societies, desires cannot serve as a guide to human behavior. Instead, with the new way of thinking, something called "necessity" (*xuyao*) serves as the justification for "plans." This shift from desire to necessity marks a very important watershed in human affairs. Let me describe the difference between the concepts of desire and necessity.

In observing human behavior, we see that human beings do not act randomly; they do not act simply for the sake of action. Actions are means to attain specific ends. Consider your own behavior. Each action has its purpose. You pick up chopsticks only when you want to eat; you fix a meal only when you want to satisfy your hunger. There is always a "want" to guide your actions. Whenever you ask others a question—such as "Why have you come?" or "What do you want?"—you can always hear in their answers their explanation for why they behave as they do. Therefore, when we talk of human behavior, we always speak of it as being motivated.

There are two implications to this belief that human behavior consists of motivated actions. One is that human beings are able to control their own behavior. If they want to do something, they do it; if they don't want to do something, they don't do it. This is what we call "will" (*yizhi*). The other meaning is that people's choices are grounded in their desires. Desires determine the direction of human behavior, the "wants" and "don't wants" that people have. These "wants" (*yao*) exist prior to behavior. When you have what you want, your desires are satisfied and you will feel happy. If your desires cannot be satisfied and you do not have what you want, you feel unhappy. In English, the word *want* expresses both "desire" and "want." The same word in English also means "to be deficient" in something. Therefore, to be deficient or to be wanting in something not only describes a state of being but also suggests a desire to attain. First comes the sensation of being uneasy, then the urge for the human body to act. This urge may be thought of as a "state of tension" (*jinzhang zhuangtai*), a condition that cannot last long and must be released in some way. Releasing the tension creates action, which brings about a sense of satisfaction in having done something. Desire, tension, action, satisfaction, happiness—these terms encompass the process underlying human behavior.

If desire controls behavior through will, actors must be conscious of their desires; self-awareness means that actors generally know what they want. There is nothing wrong with having desires, but it does raise at least one problem. Human beings may act according to their desires, but are their desires necessarily beneficial to the development of healthy individuals, or to the harmonious cooperation of individuals in society, or to the integrity and continuity of society in general? I do not raise this question to explore whether human nature is good or evil but, rather, to examine the reality of human existence. If we were to suspend our connections with the human realm for a moment and were able to stand, as it were, outside the human species in order to look at human beings as we are able to look at other animals, we would see that human beings have a very long history; they have done many things to maintain their existence and continuity. We see that they act as if healthy individual development and the integrity of society were their goals. But if we were to move closer to these people and question them, they would tell us that their many desires have nothing to do with more general social goals. Maintaining our distance from the human species, we would see men and women meeting each other, giving birth to babies, and cooperating in raising their children—all of which are necessary for the integrity of society. If no babies were born, if nobody raised children, if people died one after another, then wouldn't society be in chaos and wouldn't the human species become extinct? Thereupon, being filled with such insights, we might go to talk to couples about their long-term service to society, but they would laugh at our high-sounding conclusions and would likely say something like this: "We are together for love, not for children; the children just come along with that." Nowhere could we find people who desire only to maintain the human race. Indeed, when looking for a girlfriend, what boy would think of such bookish questions?

Similarly, still maintaining our distance from the human species, every day we see people eating carbohydrates, fats, vitamin A, and vitamin C—we could give a long list of such nutritional items. Then we could take this information back to the lab and do some research, and, sure enough, we would find that carbohydrates provide energy, that vitamin A provides this and that, and that all nutritional items combine to support life. But if we asked people who live outside modern cities why they eat pepper and garlic, they would answer, "Because they taste good, and, besides, they go with rice."

Love and good food are conscious desires. What directly decides our actions are, most certainly, those desires. But do the actions caused by desires always match the requirements for human existence? This question has sparked many scholarly discussions. If we examine the preceding paragraphs, we may come to the conclusion that human desires are quite subtle. Although human beings may want this or that, the result often exactly fulfills the needed condition for their existence. What are desires? Food and sex—they are characteristically deeply embedded in human biology. There seems to be an ingenious arrangement here: continuity is necessary for the human race, and people of different sexes fall in love; certain nutrients are necessary for life, and people like foods that have the necessary variety of nutrients. In the nineteenth century, a theory based on this kind of reasoning became widely accepted. This theory says that as long as everyone is "selfish"—that is, as long as each works entirely to satisfy the desires brought by instincts—the best and most harmonious order will emerge in society. Adam Smith saw this order—in which individuals acting for themselves would create a good life for all—as being arranged through the working of an "invisible hand."

This theory actually is based not on modern society but on a conception of rural society, because the theory is more or less correct for such a society. The reason for its correctness is not that there really is an "invisible hand" but, rather, that in rural society individual desires often do match the conditions for human existence. The two match because desires are not biological facts but cultural facts. By this I mean that people are taught to think in this way. For instance, people from northern China desire to eat garlic. This desire is not inherited but is instead learned from childhood. The "selfishness" that is a part of this theory is actually the ability to think for oneself, but the way of thinking is learned from the society. The issue is not the "want" itself, but the content of the want, and the content is determined by culture.

I maintain that desire is a cultural fact. This does not mean that all cultural facts match the requirements for human existence; many things in culture are irrelevant or even harmful to those requirements. Consider eating as an example. If all things our culture allows us to eat were in accord with nutritional principles, there would be no need for medicinal drugs. Even if we ignore drugs and other poisonous foods, ordinary food still proves the saying "Illness enters the body through the mouth" (*bing cong kou ru*). I often feel it is not very accurate to set up "survival" as an ultimate human value. If there are differences between the human race and other animals and plants, then the most important, in my view, is that humans have found values that go beyond survival, such as truth, goodness, and beauty. I like to illustrate this by saying that "humans are the only kind of animal able to commit suicide." Regardless of this fact, even though humans may have other values beyond mere survival, and even though a part of culture may be irrelevant or even harmful to human existence, a culture that does not provide the conditions necessary for its survival will be eliminated in due course, and so will the people who accept this kind of culture. Over time, they will become extinct. The reason for their gradual elimination is something not only internal to their culture but also external to it, as a part of a natural evolutionary process. This process is unrelated to values. Beauty or ugliness, goodness or evil, truths or lies—all these are irrelevant to it. This life process lays down only a few conditions; if they are fulfilled, you stay; if they are not fulfilled, you go. We should think of Xishi, so ill yet so beautiful; but nature would not allow her to live on just because of her beauty.[1] Disease leads to death; only health is the condition of survival. Nature does not prohibit people from committing suicide, but no power in nature can give life back to those who have already done so.

Another theory is relevant here. At the beginning of his famous book *Folkways*, William Graham Sumner says that for human beings action comes before ideas.[2] Action is determined by experiences accumulated through trial and error. Ideas only function to maintain those experiences over time; our conscious desires are the commands of culture. This theory is also accurate when applied to rural society. The reason is that rural society is traditional; it is a society based on the accumulation of experiences. These accumulated experiences arise out of a process of "natural selection"; "errors"—actions that do not fulfill the requirements for survival—are eliminated, so that society increasingly develops a set of time-tested recipes for living life. No matter what actors might say about them, these recipes must be beneficial to human existence.

At this point, I should stress that many actions occurring in rural society—actions that seemed to be directed toward some concrete goal or to satisfy some specific desire—turn out, on closer and more objective examination, to have no connection to their stated purpose and are not directed to satisfying the subject's perceived needs. Sorcery is the best example of this kind of behavior. In fact, to drive away a ghost is to drive away the fear in one's own heart. Whether there are ghosts or not is unimportant, but the fear has to be driven away.

In rural society, culture shapes desires; and desires, in turn, guide behavior. The result is that desires and ensuing behavior fulfill the

1. Xishi is a renowned beauty who lived during the Warring States period (480–221 B.C.).

2. William Graham Sumner, *Folkways* (New Haven, Conn.: Yale University Press, 1906).

requirements for existence. But this match between behavior and social continuity is neither conscious nor planned. The match is a subtle one and can be said to be the work of heaven (*tiangong*) in that it does not flow directly from human will, even though culture is certainly a human creation. This unconscious match between behavior and continuity has its disadvantages. When the environment changes, rural people are unable to make active plans for adapting to the changes. As Sumner said, people, proceeding blindly, are forced through trial and error to find new ways. Fortunately, the rural environment does not change very much, and the speed of that change is not very fast. Therefore, normally, people have time to make their blind tests, and the losses from their errors are usually not fatal. In the initial stage of the industrial revolution, thinkers could still conceive of a social order that was run by an "invisible hand." And, as a matter of fact, even today, in a culture as advanced and a society as complicated as the one in the United States, there is still a strong predisposition to oppose planned economies. But it is dangerous to maintain this laissez-faire spirit, which has been nurtured all along in rural society. If something goes wrong, it will be no small matter.

When society changes fast and the original culture can no longer guarantee satisfaction in life, people have to examine the relationship between their behavior and their goals. They then discover that desires are not a final motivation to action but, rather, serve as a vehicle for society to fulfill the conditions for its existence. It is then that people begin to pay attention to the conditions of existence. In sociology, a new concept appears: the concept of "function." Function means "the effect of a set of actions on the existence of individuals and the integrity of society." Social actors are not necessarily aware of functions. That is the reason we need functional analysis. Functions are like nutrition in food, rather than taste. At this point, people become consciously aware of the conditions necessary for their existence, and they talk of "necessities" as opposed to "desires." People in modern societies have begun to choose food for the sake of nutrition. This is the era of reason, and reason means that people plan their actions according to a known relationship between means and ends. Therefore, this can also be called a scientific era.

In modern society, knowledge is power. This is so because people in society make plans according to their needs. In rural society, people depend on experience and do not need to plan. This is so because, in the process of time, nature has selected for them a traditional life design on which they have come to rely. Each simply acts according to his or her own desires.

Epilogue
Sociology and the Reconstruction of Rural China

by Gary G. Hamilton and Wang Zheng

Fei wrote *Xiangtu chongjian* (Reconstructing rural China) at the same time that he was writing *Xiangtu Zhongguo*. *Xiangtu chongjian* also first appeared as essays published in newspapers and periodicals. In these essays, instead of providing an ideal-typical analysis of Chinese society, Fei offered solutions to political and economic problems that China was facing in 1948. The two books, however, are directly related in the sense that Fei's proposals were based on his sociological theories of Chinese society. The linkage between the two books is so obvious that they have been frequently published as a set.[1]

Even though chapters appear in different places, much of *Reconstructing Rural China* has been previously translated.[2] Therefore, we will not provide a translation here. Nonetheless, a brief look at Fei's proposals for rural reforms as he developed them in *Reconstructing Rural China* will help deepen our understanding of Fei's sociological vision of China and will also demonstrate the usefulness of sociological analysis in making policy decisions about economic development.

In the People's Republic of China, Fei's proposals were bitterly

1. For a publication history of *Xiangtu chongjian*, see R. David Arkush, *Fei Xiaotong and Sociology in Revolutionary China* (Cambridge, Mass.: Harvard University Press, 1981), p. 332.
2. The third, fifth, seventh, and eighth chapters have been translated in *China's Gentry: Essays in Rural-Urban Relations* (Chicago: University of Chicago Press, 1953); the tenth, eleventh, and twelfth chapters, in "Problems of Rural Industrialization," *China Economist* 1, no. 4 (April 26, 1949): 102–9; the thirteenth chapter and the epilogue, in "Financing Rural Industrialization," *China Economist* 2, no. 5 (August 1, 1948): 108–13.

criticized.[3] In the Republic of China on Taiwan, however, industrialization followed the sequence recommended by Fei's writings: comprehensive land reform, creation of public industries in some capital-intensive sectors, and heavy reliance on family enterprises for the full development of industrialization. Because Fei remained on the mainland after the 1949 revolution, his writings were officially restricted in Taiwan, although they were readily available on the black market. Therefore, Chiang Kai-shek's economic advisers certainly would not have openly mentioned that they had been influenced by Fei's proposals or even that they had read Fei's books. Even so, many Guomindang (Nationalist Party) intellectuals, being concerned and educated men, must have known about Fei's writings. Moreover, Fei's proposals for postwar reforms also might have some applicability in a post-Maoist PRC.

As its title suggests, *Reconstructing Rural China* demonstrates Fei's great concern with China's recovery in the crucial postwar period. Like most intellectuals of the time, Fei was keenly aware that China was experiencing a great historical transformation. Traditional society had to be reformed to answer the challenges of the time. But unlike many others, who were eager to replace Chinese culture with Western values and ideologies, Fei paid close attention to the existing cultural and socioeconomic conditions and cautioned people about the negative consequences of radical reforms. He laid out his goals for *Reconstructing Rural China* as follows:

> I attempt to point out how various cultural elements work together to create our traditional small farming economy. This attempt is to understand our traditional culture, not necessarily to preserve it. On the contrary, this is exactly the kind of knowledge on which effective reform must be based. One cannot reform a culture by starting a new culture from scratch. Nor can one form a culture by creating it in a void and then simply applying that abstract plan to our situation. To reform a culture is to weed out the old in order to let the new emerge. The new has to grow from the old. Of course, historical continuity is a burden to reformers anxiously wanting to change society. But, in reality, the old things and the old customs that have been a drag on new cultural developments cannot be avoided. These are objective limitations which must be faced. We

3. See the discussion of this criticism in our introductory chapter.

achieve freedom only when we recognize those limitations. Moreover, recognizing limitations does not mean submitting to them; rather, it is a necessary step toward overcoming them, because we then know both ourselves and our enemies. . . . Like strategy in warfare, design in architecture, and diagnosis in medicine, cultural reforms also need a rational plan, and cultural analysis is the basis for such plans.[4]

Arguing that careful objective analysis comes before, and lays the foundation for, the task of planning reforms, Fei concentrates his recommendations in two broad areas needing the most change: politics and the economy.

TWO-TRACK POLITICS

Fei's recommendations for political reforms are based on his scholarly conclusion that Chinese political institutions rest on a "two-track" system.[5] Fei develops the theoretical basis for this conclusion in *Xiangtu Zhongguo* (chapters 8–11), where he argues that rural society is largely self-regulating. He observes that Chinese traditional political structure was organized at two different and distinct levels: the level of the central government and the level of local society. What the central government is able to do at the local level is very limited, because local affairs are actually run by informal local networks headed by the gentry. As a consequence, China historically developed a two-track political system. One track goes from the top down, whereby the official bureaucracy, carrying orders from the emperor, tries to influence society in a variety of ways and with various degrees of success. The other track goes from the bottom up. At the local level, which is largely autonomous from a state system, notables exercise their influence and put pressure on higher-level officials and, in the past, would even petition the emperor in order to protect local interests. Generally speaking, however, local people hardly had any contact with the central government; to them, "Heaven is high and the emperor is far away."

In *Reconstructing Rural China*, Fei further argues that in tradi-

4. *Xiangtu chongjian* (Xianggang: Wenxue chubanshe, n.d.), pp. 151–52. The translation here, and elsewhere in this chapter, is ours.
5. Ibid., pp. 44–49.

tional times there were two lines of defense preventing the emperors from obtaining dictatorial power: first, the local autonomy gained from the "gentry buffer," and, second, the preference for inaction (*wuwei*) in Chinese political philosophy.[6] However, in modern times, both lines of defense were broken. Policies advocating inaction were discarded, because the complex political and economic problems of the nineteenth and early twentieth centuries required an active, powerful central government. Fei believed that a more powerful central government was inevitable. But what he bemoaned was the destruction of local autonomy.

The *baojia* system—a system of mutual household supervision—that the Republican government had developed from earlier precedents attempted to extend the central government's power from the county level, where it had been previously delimited, into each household. Officials were selected and sent by the government into villages. The new political powers did not replace the old autonomous associations that were so effective at the local level, but they did cause a loss of legitimacy. Therefore, Fei felt that central power was consolidated but that the political track from the bottom to the top became less effective, if not blocked altogether. The central government tried to destroy "the fulcrum to the traditional balance between centralized and decentralized power, . . . the safety valve against dictatorship."[7] As a result of this imbalance, inefficiency and corruption became widespread in local administration.

Fei made it clear that what he advocated was not a restoration of the traditional system of two-track politics. In traditional society, most gentry were landlords, a parasitical group. Because they had influential social connections and stood at the center of the local network structures, they could easily abuse their powers and oppress the common people. Moreover, the gentry were not always effective in checking imperial power, because their influence worked only through informal organizations and social connections. When these were not present for some reason, imperial power would become more oppressive. Finally, gentry power was by no means a democracy in which the interests of the people were represented

6. Ibid., pp. 44–46, 54–64. The thesis is also found in *China's Gentry*, chaps. 1 and 4.

7. Ibid., pp. 52, 53.

to higher-level authorities. The gentry, rather, were interested in their own power and their own positions.

Fei did not recommend that the gentry be strengthened, but he did recommend that, in view of an increasingly centralized and powerful government, China should somehow consolidate the bottom-up political track. What needed to be restored was local autonomy, and what needed to be created was a new local leadership consisting of people other than the gentry. Fei envisioned a great transformation of the political system emerging out of traditional Chinese political institutions: "The imperial power will change into a central administration responsible to the people; gentry power, into legislative representatives elected by the people; bureaucrats, into public servants in an efficient civilian government; factional power, into industrial, commercial, and occupational organizations. And the entire political structure will rest on the foundation provided by local consent power."[8]

Fei did not discuss in detail the procedures of this huge transformation. As he admitted, he did not have direct answers for how to achieve the transformation. His insights on the dangers of centralized government in a Chinese context are persuasive, but he offered no answers for developing a system of checks and balances to prevent centralization.

His lack of direct answers can be attributed, in part, to the difficulty of solving the major problem in designing a democratic system for China: Who would become the new leaders of local society for China's vast countryside? Chinese peasants had been under authoritarian rule for thousands of years. It would be unrealistic, he argued, to expect peasants suddenly to develop a concept of modern citizenship. As an alternative, Fei expressed hope that— just as in England, where retired professionals returned to their hometowns and became involved in local affairs[9]—Chinese intellectuals would return to their hometowns and play a leading role in the transitional period. But Fei was not optimistic on this score.

In traditional society, scholars were scattered in rural and urban areas, and those who successfully passed the imperial examinations would eventually return to their hometowns, where they could

8. Ibid., p. 163.
9. Ibid., pp. 59–61.

assume an elite position in local society. But in recent Chinese history, rural areas gradually lost human resources. Educated people no longer returned to their hometowns. Fei saw this phenomenon as the effect of Westernization on China. Cities became the places where Chinese culture encountered Western culture. In a short time, cultural differences between Chinese urban and rural areas increased substantially. People living in urban centers were influenced by, and became accustomed to, Western values and life-styles; as a result, urbanites became alienated from rural society and its values—the very values that, in Fei's view, embodied Chinese tradition and could provide a basis for modernizing reforms. Even if educated young people wished to return to their hometowns, they would find that what they had learned in modern schools had nothing to do with rural life. Modern education was imported from the West and emphasized scientific and other types of technical knowledge, rather than rituals and social norms as the traditional schools had done. Fei maintained that the gap between Western scientific knowledge and Chinese rural reality had, somehow, to be bridged.

For educated people to be useful in rural areas, Fei proposed two approaches. First, teachers should make modern education useful in the everyday lives of rural people; education should be practical. Second, new enterprises that required modern knowledge should be created in villages, so that people with a modern education would want to go and work there.

RURAL INDUSTRY

Fei's discussion of political reform inevitably led to an examination of economic patterns. As he told Burton Pasternak decades later, he had already assumed, even before he knew about Marxism, that basic economic activity—production—molds ideas. He was convinced early in his life that only a changed economic structure would be able to change peasant mentality.[10] The major part of *Recon-*

10. In the interview with Pasternak ("A Conversation with Fei Xiaotong," *Current Anthropology* 29, no. 4 [Aug–Oct. 1988]: 655), Fei observed that for peasants "the first priority is not democracy, they need security first. . . . We must move away from a peasant mentality. Unless the 80% of China's population that are small farmers change their occupation, China will continue to be crippled."

structing Rural China is devoted to issues of the rural economy.[11] As a sociologist who had done many field studies in rural areas, Fei felt deeply that the rural impoverishment of his time had to be remedied. His view of China's future economic structure, therefore, was expressed as a diagnosis of rural impoverishment and prescriptions to remedy it.

Fei developed his thesis on rural impoverishment when he wrote *Peasant Life in China*: because of China's large population and scarce arable land, the rural economy was sustained by subsidiary occupations. The crops from the land barely supported the livelihood of peasant families and left no surplus value to pay rent to the landlord or taxes to the government; but with the income from household and handicraft industries, the traditional land system was able to survive. When Western industries poured their products into the Chinese market, however, rural handicraft industries declined and the rural economy became based solely on agricultural production. Because crops from land could not support both peasants and landlords, peasant life deteriorated, even though the landlords did not raise their rent.

The solutions to the problem were, Fei proposed, land reform and a revival of rural industry. Fei based his proposal on his theoretical analysis of rural society. In *Xiangtu Zhongguo* (chapters 6, 7, and 12), he observed that the family, conceptualized as the "small lineage," was the "medium through which all activities are organized" in local society and was a highly disciplined force. Using this observation, Fei proposed to make the family the key unit of social change in China's drive for industrialization.

In *Reconstructing Rural China*, Fei's plan for land reform called for landlords to give up their privileges and return land to peasant families, and for the government to provide limited compensation in the form of bonds to the landlords so that they could shift their resources into industry, thereby becoming a productive class rather than a parasitical one. Fei emphasized that the exploitative land system had to be eliminated but that the landlords could be transformed into productive social groups. "If the landlord class could

---

11. *Xiangtu chongjian* consists of thirteen chapters with an introduction and an answer to readers' criticisms at the end of the book. Of the thirteen articles, seven are on the rural economy.

not find a new productive economic basis, they would not easily give up their land. Therefore, the ideal of peasant proprietorship may have to be realized by violent rather than consensual means. . . . My position is to attempt to find a peaceful solution to this fundamental problem that must be dealt with immediately." [12]

Reforming the land system, however, would solve only one aspect of rural impoverishment. Although it would eliminate rent as a major expenditure in peasant households, that alone would not be enough to revive the rural economy. To do that, Fei thought, it was vital to build rural industry. Almost half of the book is devoted to this one important issue.

Fei had three recommendations for how to revitalize rural industry. The first recommendation was to improve the peasants' standard of living. The huge population and the scarcity of arable land made it very difficult for peasants to have any substantial increase in income simply by farming. But if peasants could grow some kind of crop, such as silkworms or cotton, that would require further processing, and if that processing could be done in the villages, surplus rural labor could be utilized and family income increased.

The second recommendation was to build Chinese industrialization on a rural foundation. Fei maintained that industrialization in China should be different from that in the West. Chinese industry should not concentrate in urban areas. No urban industrial area could absorb such a huge rural population. Urban industry might be able to develop quickly with a concentration of investment and technology, but rural poverty would remain the same or worsen. In the long run, rural poverty would hinder the growth of urban industry, because the huge rural population could not provide a market for the industrial products made in the cities. Moreover, cheap rural labor might give China some initial advantages in competing with products coming from advanced Western industry.

By advocating rural industry, Fei did not mean that all indus-

---

12. *Xiangtu chongjian*, p. 89. Although Fei thought that he was suggesting rational means toward a rational end, he was later accused, in the 1950s, of protecting landlord interests. The proposal of peaceful land reform, contrary to methods of the Communist Party, got him into much trouble. Ironically, this means-ends calculus seems to have been accepted by the Nationalist Party on Taiwan and to have greatly aided Taiwan's economic development.

tries should be moved to the countryside. Rather, he specifically recommended that light industry, handicrafts, and other types of small-scale production that did not require either high technology or heavy investment could be scattered throughout rural areas.

The third recommendation was to avoid a monopoly of new technology and a concentration of social wealth in the hands of the few. Industrialization in the West had produced a new privileged class. Such a class was contrary to Fei's idea that technology should benefit all the people. He noticed that some industrialized countries, such as England, had adopted socialism as a means to channel social wealth obtained from industry into backward rural areas. Fei thought, however, that this kind of indirect redistribution of wealth would not serve China well, regardless of the type of government China eventually developed. Small-scale industries were typically so politically weak and impoverished that, without direct gains, peasants would not be able to shoulder the burden of developing a rural infrastructure. Therefore, a direct share in the profits of industrialization was more beneficial and more realistic.

The organization of rural industry in Fei's design was again a modified version of the traditional patterns. In traditional Chinese society, there had been two basic forms of enterprises: household enterprises and workshops in villages and towns. Although they were an important part of the rural economy, both had their faults. On the one hand, household enterprises, limited by capital and labor, could take on only a very narrow range of small-scale industries. Moreover, peasants would be severely exploited if they sold their products through middlemen. On the other hand, workshops located in small cities could engage in larger and more complex industries, but such workshops were usually owned by only a few elite families.

Considering these shortcomings, Fei recommended a new form of organization: cooperatives composed of many household enterprises. The cooperatives would allow peasants to engage in big projects while retaining their traditional patterns of household-based organization. More important, peasants would become owners of the collective enterprise and share the profits directly. Increasing the size and complexity of these rural enterprises could also increase production efficiency and introduce some elements of centralized management. Like the traditional workshops, cooperative factories could be built in villages and towns; but, unlike the traditional workshops, they would have collective ownership. Fei summarized this point as follows: "What I call rural industry includes the following elements: (1) Peasant families participate in industry without giving up farming. (2) The location of industries is scattered in and around villages. (3) Such industries belong to the peasants who participate in them; therefore, ownership is cooperative. (4) The raw material for such industries is mainly produced by the peasants themselves. (5) Most important, the profits from the industry are directly distributed to the peasants."[13]

Discussing the ways of accumulating capital for China's industrialization, Fei made a prophetic analysis about what might happen in China. He opposed the idea that a central government should concentrate capital through compulsory savings. He admitted that such compulsory savings would provide fast accumulation, and perhaps even effective use, of capital. However, Fei warned of the political consequences that would follow if such a policy were adopted in China:

> If we give such power to the government, we must first guarantee that it will not abuse the power and will not become even more corrupted than the landlords. . . . In a time when people are not yet capable of checking government power, further increasing government power must tempt the power holders to abuse their position. . . . In a country with backward industries and with people who have comparatively little political sophistication, it is very likely that a powerful centralized government will emerge. Such a government will use its political power to accumulate capital and to plan industry. After the economic base is stabilized, political freedoms and other such rights that are secondary to sheer survival could be discussed and enacted, but it would be very lucky if this happened in such a country, because it would be a miracle for powers that are beyond people's control suddenly to start serving the people. Miracles may occur, of course, but they cannot be taken for granted. In order to guarantee that the government will serve the people, people will first have to check the power of government. This is the normal way with politics. In order to avoid the emergence of bureaucratic capitalism and of dictatorship, I have to be suspicious of government compulsory savings programs and government-operated industries.[14]

13. *Xiangtu chongjian*, pp. 103–4.
14. Ibid., pp. 138–40.

Fei pointed out that there are no guarantees that the government will be capable of making wise investments with the money collected from the people. "A country without industrial experience is hardly capable of creating state-run enterprises."[15]

Eloquently outlining the faults of an industry run by a powerful centralized government, Fei elaborated the feasibility and significance of rural industry. Again he applied his sociological analysis to this project. Fei pointed out that in Chinese traditional culture, to glorify one's family was a value, and in rural society the most powerful motivation was to establish family property. Chinese people might be more willing to work hard and live a frugal life if they were benefiting their families rather than their government. For people to save voluntarily and to achieve a satisfactory level of efficiency, therefore, Fei advocated promoting family-run enterprises. Rural industry based on household enterprises was congruent with Chinese cultural values and Chinese social psychology. "I do not suggest that we should stop at family production," Fei said. "But I think this is the most reliable starting point and also the most reliable foundation."[16]

It has been more than forty years since Fei made the above proposals for rural reforms, and only now have rural industries become a significant part of the mainland economy. After the Cultural Revolution, Fei continued his rural research, and still today he is one of the most prominent advocates for rural industrialization. Since 1982, he has conducted a national research project on the development of small towns and rural industries.[17] He frequently publishes papers on his research and serves as an influential adviser on issues of rural development.

The past fifteen years of economic reforms in China seem to vindicate Fei's vision. In most parts of China, peasant households are now free to make decisions on how to farm the small pieces of

15. Ibid., p. 139.
16. Ibid., p. 143.
17. For an account of Fei's recent work, see "Xiao chengzhen diaocha zishu" (A talk on the study of small towns), in *Fei Xiaotong xueshu jinghua lu* (The best academic writings of Fei Xiaotong) (Beijing: Shifan University Press, 1988), pp. 127–40. In this article, Fei summarizes the importance of rebuilding small towns. Making small towns into political, economic, and cultural centers in the rural areas, he thinks, would not only strengthen the rural economy but also attract intellectuals to the rural area. Here Fei expresses his convictions formed forty years ago and proposes a solution to the problem of rural "brain drain."

land allocated to them. Chinese peasants have found ways to use their surplus labor, primarily in subsidiary industries and handicrafts. Family enterprises and cooperative factories in villages and towns have flourished in recent years, and peasant life has improved substantially for the first time in nearly forty years. Although some setbacks, including a severe recession, have occurred and the pace of rural development has slowed as a result, we believe nonetheless that Fei's pattern of rural development will survive, just as Fei's sociology survived forty years of the Maoist line.

While his project for rural industry has materialized in part, Fei's double-track politics has never been a reality. Though the concept has been much discussed in academic circles in recent years, China is still ruled through a centralized state subject to little if any control by those outside the inner sphere of government. The line of defense against a centralized dictatorship, which Fei advocated forty years ago, has not yet been built. Since 1949, those who have advocated more say in government have been persecuted, imprisoned, and sometimes put to death. Though Fei himself is now an influential person within several government circles, he has not pursued this sensitive topic in recent years.

Glossary

ai 愛

baojia 保甲
Baoqin 寶琴
baozhang 保長
bing cong kou ru 病從口入
bu shi qi lun 不失其倫
bu zhi lao zhi jiang zhi 不知老之
　將至

chaxugeju 差序格局
Chen Sheng 陳勝
Chi 赤

da jiating 大家庭
di 地
diwei 地位
diyuan 地緣

fali 法理
Feng Xiaoqing 馮小青
fu bu fu, zi bu zi 父不父, 子不子
fu er hao li 富而好禮

gang 綱
ganqing 感情
Gaoyao 皋陶
guanxi 關係
Gui Youguang 歸有光

hanren 漢人
hedi guanglin 闔第光臨

Jia 賈
jia 家
jialide 家里的
jiamen 家門
Jiangcun 江村
jiguan 籍貫
jiji 寄籍
Jing hua yuan 鏡花緣
jinzhang zhuangtai 緊張狀態

ke 克
ke ji fu li 克己復禮
kebian 客邊
kongjian 空間
kuaishou 快手

li 里
li 禮
liaojie 瞭解
Liji 禮記
Lin Daiyu 林黛玉
lingyan 靈驗
lisu 禮俗
Lucun 祿村
lun 倫

153

Meiguo renxingge 美國人性格

Meng Wubo 孟武伯

mianduimian 面對面

Pan Guangdan 潘光旦

pingli 評理

qianhui 錢會

qingsuan 清算

Qiu 求

ren 仁

renlun 人倫

renqing 人情

sangang 三綱

shehui guanxi 社會關係

shehui quanzi 社會圈子

Shengyu zhidu 生育制度

Shiji 史記

Shiji pinglun 世紀評論

Shiming 釋名

shishi quanli 時勢權力

shizu 氏族

Shun 舜

shuren 熟人

Sima Niu 司馬牛

songshi 訟師

Su Qin 蘇秦

suanzhang 算賬

Tao Ying 桃應

tiangong 天工

tianxia 天下

tianxia zhi dadao 天下之達道

tiaojie 調解

tong 同

tongshi 同事

tongxiang 同鄉

tongxue 同學

tongzhuyi 同主義

tu 土

tuantigeju 團體格局

Tudi 土地

tui 推

tuqi 土氣

waicunren 外村人

Wan Zhang 萬章

wei zheng bu zai duo yan 爲政不在多言

wenhua yingxiong 文化英雄

Wu Guang 吳廣

wuqing 無情

wuwei er zhi 無爲而治

wuwei zhengzhi 無爲政治

xi 習

Xiang 象

Xiangjixuan ji 項脊軒記

Xiangtu chongjian 鄉土重建

Xiangtu Zhongguo 鄉土中國

xianshi 閑事

xiao 孝

xiao jiazu 小家族

Xiaojing 孝經

xin 心

xin 信

xinke 新客

Xishi 西施

Xiuyun 岫雲

xue 學

Xue Baochai　薛寶釵

xuexi　學習

xueyuan　血緣

xuyao　需要

yan bi Yao Shun　言必堯舜

Yan Yuan　顏淵

Yang Zhu　楊朱

Yao　瑤

yao　要

yi　義

yizhi　意志

yu　愚

yue　約

yuwang　欲望

zhanglao tongzhi　長老統治

zhong　忠

Zhongyong　中庸

Zigong　子貢

zijiaren　自家人

Zilu　子路

Ziwen　子文

Zizhang　子張

zong　賝

zu　族

Index